A SAIN

SHORT BIBLE CATECHISM

By
John C. Kersten, S.V.D.

Illustrated

CATHOLIC BOOK PUBLISHING CO.
NEW YORK

NIHIL OBSTAT: Aeden Manning, S.T.   *Censor Deputatus*

IMPRIMATUR: ✠ J. B. Brunini, D.D.   *Bishop of Jackson, Mississippi*

(T-225)

PREFACE

A digest. This book is a digest of the very popular "Bible Catechism." It was brought to my attention that not all students need or want to go through as thorough a course in adapted theology as the "Bible Catechism" offers.

This simplified edition, however, does not make the larger edition superfluous. The "Bible Catechism" remains a necessary resource book for teachers of religion who want to instruct or update students on what a modern Catholic believes.

The International Review of Catechetics, entitled "Lumen Vitae," has said of the "Bible Catechism" that "its content deals very successfully with the most important and oft repeated questions of Christians" (1974, no. 1, p. 127).

It is indeed a challenge for college graduates and a necessity for teachers! The ancient saying "Contemplata tradere" is still the rule: you can only teach efficiently what you have first meditated upon.

The latest. With respect to the latest in Catechetics as a science, art, or skill, I have seen new methods come and go in rapid succession. Usually they relate to the latest in school education. For some years I served as a chaplain in a European training college for school teachers, where I was exposed to the history, the presence, and the future of didactic systems. In my youthful enthusiasm, quite often uncritically, I tried out my findings on Catechetics. I wanted to offer the latest!

Perhaps it is still true that in order to have a new catechism rated favorably, which is important for its success on the market, it should reflect the latest. But is it? Certainly, each new method brings out a few aspects that were neglected in former ones. For example, inductive catechesis of experience is "in" nowadays. And rightly so. Father Edward Schillebeeckx states bluntly: "The breach between faith and experience is one of the fundamental causes of the contemporary crisis of faith" ("Righteousness and Love," p. 23).

Although theologians do not always agree on how experience and faith are interrelated, one thing is sure. The catechist should not just transfer information. Most of all, he/she must help the student to attain that participatory knowledge which with the help of God makes the Christian. And evoking experience creates conditions for the converting encounter!

A catechism is by definition a text, the biblical one included, in which persons are to be inducted through the medium of evoked experience. Hence, it must reflect this process. It cannot, however, substitute for the encounter with an inspired catechist!

The Bible. Structuralism, Theology of Story, and Process Thought can be seen in a perspective similar to what I have observed above. However, over the years I became ever more convinced that, regardless of whether or not a catechism reflects the latest methodology, it will succeed only if it makes students dedicated, intelligent, and above all prayerful Bible readers. That is why the primary goal of this catechism is the Bible. Most contemporary catechisms quote the Bible every so often, but I do not detect in them the ardent concern to make students devout Bible readers.

Though we don't favor a fundamentalist exegesis of the Bible as it is often taught by our separated brothers and sisters, we can learn from them. The Bible is *the* identity symbol which keeps them together. After Vatican II, we have done away with so many of our paradigms, which has caused a dangerous vacuum. This author is convinced that we should fill it with the paradigms of Word (Bible) and Sacrament (mainly a meaningful celebration of the Eucharist). Why not combine a great love and respect for the Bible with sound scholarship as reflected in our Catholic Bibles under guidance of the Church?

Church teaching. Don't Catholics need more than the Bible? What about the documents of the Magisterium? One Sunday afternoon I attended the Baptist funeral of the father of one of my parishioners. It was Bible and biblical discourse I heard from beginning to end. That same night I took part in a neighboring Catholic Church affair, at which the keynote speaker quoted one document of the Church after another. Not even once was the Bible mentioned.

Yet, after reading the Bible in church we say: "This is the Word of the Lord," which we do not say after reading a Church document! Catholics need to know what the Church teaches. But at least implicitly most of it is in the Bible. And a devout Bible reader will pay more attention to what Father says on Sunday morning if his sermon is a homily on the Bible readings in the perspective of Church teaching rather than the other way around. This catechism aims to be such a homily.

No handbook. Like "Bible Catechism" this book is a catechism not a handbook for the catechist. Since the experience of adults is so varied, this author does not believe in a handbook for the catechist, just as he does not favor advanced prepared sermons for the preacher.

The catechist should use a variety of material, know his/her students and their world, and correlate all of it to this text and the experience of God's people as reflected in the Bible. A religious instruction requires as meticulous a preparation as a Sunday sermon does.

Language. Structural Language Analysis teaches that language is an essential part of experience. That is why I have tried to translate a traditional and often outdated religious idiom into that of the modern Catholic.

I invite the colleague who glances over this Preface and ponders using the book, or having it used by his/her teachers, to read Father Avery Dulles' book "A Church to Believe In" (Crossroads Books, 1982), Chapter 8: "The Two Magisteria," especially pp. 128-132, before he condemns this catechism as another novelty.

Catechumenate—Mystagogia. For working with candidates who intend to join the Church, I might suggest using this book. for the Catechumenate proper (. . . to Easter). For the Mystagogia (Easter to Pentecost) I suggest using my book "Bible Meditations for Every Day" (Catholic Book Publishing Co.).

John C. Kersten, SVD

CONTENTS

1. AN EXPERIENCE

1. Power of images. Psychology teaches us that in the process of growing up we were influenced by images, mental pictures of people around us, more than by abstract statements about what to do and not to do. A list of do's and don'ts does not impress a young person, but examples do. When in 1979 Pope John Paul II "celebrated" with the youngsters of New York City, one said: "He must be a good guy because he is concerned about people." Mother Teresa of Calcutta captivates the whole world. She won the Nobel Prize in 1979, and while other communities of Sisters dwindle her community has grown to 1800 dedicated followers in the last decade.

In your own life, think of your parents, teachers, possibly a priest, or any other good person! Without denying the function of your genes, we are justified in asserting that by relating to them you have become the person that you are right now.

2. Abraham, model of faith. Apparently, the writers of the Bible knew all this without the benefit of modern psychology. Inspired by God, they teach us by referring to models that we are invited to follow. One such model is Abraham, called "our father in faith." You may read about him in Genesis 12–23 and Paul's commentary on these narratives which is found in Romans 4:18-25.

Read these passages meditatively. Pause every so often and ask yourself: "What does this mean to me?" And always respond in spontaneous prayer!

3. Faith—a disclosure experience. Did you ever fall in love? Did you ever "see" a person the way you never saw him/her before, so that he/she became a friend? Psychologists call this "a disclosure experience." It is an experience for which you can give some reasons but which you cannot fully explain to an outsider. It is a gift.

A disclosure experience of the "Ultimate Reality— the Ground of your Being" as a loving person, a father, is called faith. You have some reasons for being "in faith," but you cannot fully explain it. It is a gift of God.

4. Abraham's experience of God. Abraham had this type of experience. In Biblical language it is described as "God appeared to Abraham—God spoke to Abraham—an angel of the Lord said . . . ." In contemporary language we would say: "Abraham experienced God as present to him." Look for this in Genesis 12–13.

The Lord Jesus had a similar experience time and again. The Gospels tell about it and we will discuss Jesus' experience of God as "Abba—Father" in its proper place later on.

5. Prayerful Bible reading. In faith we follow these models described in the Bible. Pray often: "God, give me the faith of Abraham, and that of the Lord Jesus! Help me to grow in faith."

Read and pray your Bible constantly. Just as love can be kept alive only by constant communication with the person you love, so your faith can be kept alive only by regular prayerful Bible reading. (See also pp. 96-97.)

6. Bible reading

The Power of Faith

Hoping against hope, Abraham believed and so became the father of many nations, just as it was once told him, "Numerous as this shall your descendants be." Without growing weak in faith he thought of his own body, which was as good as dead (for he was nearly a hundred years old), and of the dead womb of Sarah. Yet he never questioned or doubted God's promise; rather, he was strengthened in faith and gave glory to God, fully persuaded that God could do whatever he had promised. Thus his faith was credited to him as justice.

The words, "It was credited to him," were not written with him alone in view; they were intended for us too. For our faith will be credited to us also if we believe in him who raised Jesus our Lord from the dead, the Jesus who was handed over to death for our sins and raised up for our justification.

(Romans 4:18-25)

Questions for Discussion

1. Discuss the persons who have given direction to your life. Why did they impress you so much?

2. In the narratives about Abraham, what impresses you?

3. What is love? What is faith? How are love and faith related?

2. LET MY PEOPLE GO

1. Liberators of peoples. Heroic freedom fighters have always captivated the imagination of those who are open to a challenge: for example, George Washington, who set Americans free, and Abraham Lincoln, who opened the path to freedom for a minority that had been kept in slavery in our land of the free. Similar liberators were Gandhi, who led his people to freedom from the British by non-violence, and Dr. Martin Luther King, who did the same in this country.

These great men were controversial. They were simultaneously loved and hated. But history has vindicated them.

2. Jesus—Liberator of the human spirit. The George Washington of the Hebrews is Moses. Read about him in Exodus. This freedom fighter has captivated the imagination of generations of Hebrews to such an extent that he and the exodus from Egypt became a paradigm (model) for liberation from all evil and sin.

Matthew even describes Jesus as a new Moses, whom he portrays as persecuted by an evil king (like Moses in his earliest infancy), as coming out of Egypt (like Moses), and thus as a great prophet (spokesman) of God, liberating people from sin and evil by his life, death and resurrection. Read Matthew 2.

3. Freedom for growth in love of God. Liberation from evil (sin and vices within us: selfishness, envy, hatred, prejudice, indifference to those we should love, addiction to alcohol or drugs) is a negative value. Once free, what now? Moses and his Hebrews, who came out of Egypt, had to face this question: What now?

Their reflection on this theme bore fruit. The time of wandering in the desert became a time of growing awareness of being free *for* the beautiful relationship of human beings with God: the covenant, that partnership of love. God is the bridegroom and His people is the bride.

In later reflection, this awareness of God, lovingly present to human beings, will grow. Read about it in Isaiah 54:4-10. We will refer to it more than once, because that awareness should grow in you all the time. You either grow in awareness of God, lovingly present to us, or your relationship with Him withers.

Check yourself! What vices in you keep you a captive, not free for a total self-surrender in love to God? Pray for freedom from what is evil in you in order to be free for loving God, in Whom you live and move and have your being.

4. Bible reading

God proposes His Covenant

In the third month after their departure from the land of Egypt on its first day, the Israelites came to the desert of Sinai. After the journey from Rephidim to the desert of Sinai, they pitched camp.

While Israel was encamped here in front of the mountain, Moses went up the mountain to God. Then the Lord called to him and said, "Thus shall you say to the house of Jacob; tell the Israelites: You have seen for yourselves how I treated the Egyptians and how I bore you up on eagle wings and brought you here to myself. Therefore, if you hearken to my voice and keep my covenant, you shall be my special possession, dearer to me than all other people, though all the earth is mine. You shall be to me a kingdom of priests, a holy nation. This is what you must tell the Israelites."   *(Exodus 19:1-6)*

Questions for Discussion

1. Why is a person in the grip of vices not free to love? Discuss examples!

2. What is the negative and what is the positive side of freedom?

3. What can you learn from the Hebrews' desert experience?

3. AND HIS KINGDOM WILL HAVE NO END

1. The legendary kingdom of Arthur. When the Romans departed from Britain, they left behind them a land that soon broke up into numerous dukedoms with petty kings fighting one another. It was the legendary King Arthur who brought all these tribal chiefs together and united them into one kingdom of peace and prosperity.

Later in English literature, Arthur was ever more idealized and became the great King Arthur we read about in high school. Camelot, the place where King Arthur had his palace and court, became the nostalgic paradigm for many a politician's program, John F. Kennedy among them.

2. The idealized kingdom of David. The King Arthur of the Hebrews was King David. He united the tribes of Israel into a strong and prosperous kingdom. (See 2 Samuel 5.) Like King Arthur, he was idealized in

15

the literature of his people (the Bible) ever more. And when the Hebrews were oppressed and humiliated by mighty neighbors, they nostalgically dreamt about their past and begged God to restore the kingdom of David.

Hence, a freedom fighter who would defeat the Babylonians, Syrians, Greeks or Romans had to be of David's lineage. Moreover, keep in mind that in Hebrew thought a new king became a son of God, God's representative on earth, at the moment of his enthronement. An inauguration song still known to us brings this out clearly. Read Isaiah 9:1-6. For more on King David, read 2 Samuel.

3. The spiritual Kingdom of God. The theologians of the New Testament describe the Christian movement for a better world as "the Kingdom of God," a kingdom of love and justice in the hearts of all human beings. Jesus Christ is the king of that Kingdom, God's Son, His representative on earth. And the inauguration song of Isaiah 9:1-6 is applied to Him.

Consequently, Jesus as king is regarded as coming from Davidic lineage (read Luke 1:32-33), and David's legendary kingdom becomes the paradigm of God's Kingdom on earth with Jesus as universal king.

4. God's Kingdom found in the Catholic Church. Where do we find that Kingdom (Reign) of God with Jesus as king? We find it in the Catholic Church. This does not mean that we don't find it in the Churches that are separated from us and in the hearts of all people of good will.

Together with all who seek Christ sincerely, consciously or unconsciously, be it in separation or in error, we establish the Church in her full sense. And in this sinful and divided Church we find the Kingdom or elements of it.

5. God's Kingdom in us. Establishing God's Reign on earth should be the concern of all Christians. Start with yourself. It is worthwhile to be obedient to Christ whose yoke is gentle and burden light.

Read the Bible passages meditatively, apply them to your own life situation, and respond in spontaneous prayer. Reading the Bible simply for the sake of information is boring and missing the point. Ask your instructor to help you.

6. Bible reading

The Kingship of Jesus

Pilate went back into the praetorium and summoned Jesus. "Are you the King of the Jews?" he asked him. Jesus answered, "Are you saying this on your own, or have others been telling you about me?" "I am no Jew!" Pilate retorted. "It is your own people and the chief priests who have handed you over to me. What have you done?" Jesus answered:

"My kingdom does not belong to this world. If my kingdom were of this world, my subjects would be fighting to save me from being handed over to the Jews. As it is, my kingdom is not here."

At this Pilate said to him, "So, then, you are a king?" Jesus replied:

"It is you who say I am a king. The reason I was born, the reason why I came into the world, is to testify to the truth. Anyone committed to the truth hears my voice."   *(John 18:33-37)*

Questions for Discussion

1. Why did Hebrew thought regard every freedom fighter as somehow related to King David?
2. Why did David's kingdom become the paradigm (model) for Jesus' kingdom of God?
3. Where do we find the kingdom of God?

4. EUCHARIST — THANKSGIVING

1. Experiencing God in creation. Did you ever take a brisk walk in the early morning of a beautiful day in spring? The sky azure, trees budding and clothing themselves in the most tender green, birds chirping, and a squirrel elegantly climbing a tree? Did you ever gaze at a clear sky at night, watching the thousands of stars quietly blinking from outer space? And did you ever experience in all this your Maker?

2. Thanksgiving to our Creator. The Hebrews experienced God in nature and prayed: "How manifold are your works, O Lord! In wisdom you have wrought them all" (Psalm 104:24). The writer of the first chapter of Genesis brings this out in his well-known poem. In six portions he sums up whatever he sees, calls these portions days and has God rest on the seventh day, thus telling you and me that we should reserve one day a week to thank our Maker.

We do this every Sunday when we celebrate the Eucharist—Thanksgiving—Mass. Read Genesis 1 and pray in response Psalm 148: "Praise the Lord from the heavens."

3. God's manner of communicating with us. The ancient Hebrews were aware of God mainly as transcending His creation, living high up over the firmament. Their concept of God was conditioned by a primitive understanding of the earth. So was their awareness of God as the king of the universe communicating with the human race.

THE WORLD OF THE HEBREWS
Heavenly Seat of the Divinity

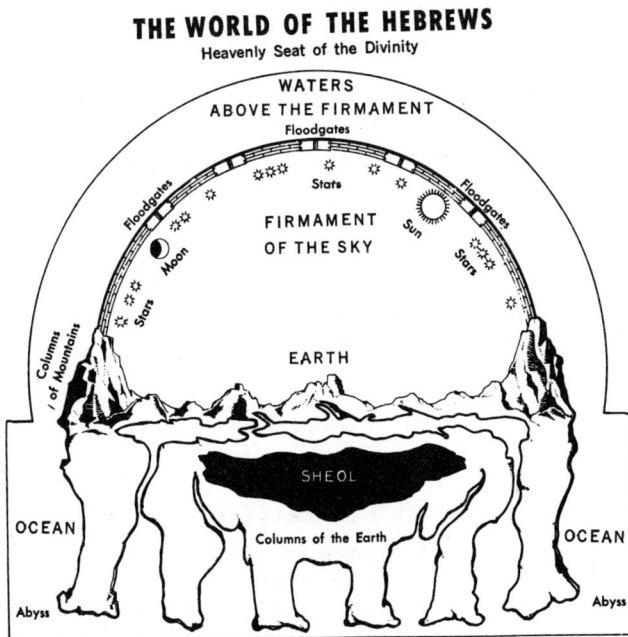

In those days, kings did not communicate with their people through newspapers, radio, or television. They used messengers—angels. Hence, the great King "up there" constantly had angels—messengers going down to deliver messages to humankind.

Today, God may not use angels, but he certainly uses fellow human beings to speak to us. Whenever you read in the Bible, "an angel of the Lord said...," think of God communicating with you—in Scripture, a sermon, the

Liturgy (worship service), any good person, music, the beauty of nature—and expecting an answer, i.e., your prayer!

4. Co-workers of God. Note also that the sacred writer of Genesis discusses extensively how God orders the chaos (un-organized matter) into a habitable world and how He chose human beings as His co-workers. Whether humans are inventing the wheel in ancient times or building today's chemical plants, computers, and spacecrafts, they are God's co-workers.

When you are repairing a car, giving birth to a child, cooking a meal for the family, or studying in school, you are creatively busy fashioning the chaos (unordered or less ordered matter) into a better world! Artists are especially conscious and proud of their creativity; but all can have these same sentiments, particularly when creatively occupied in education, molding and fashioning children into better men and women.

5. Bible reading

Praise the Lord of Creation

May the glory of the Lord endure forever;
    may the Lord be glad in his works!
He who looks upon the earth, and it trembles;
    who touches the mountains, and they smoke!
I will sing to the Lord all my life;
    I will sing praise to my God while I live.   *(Psalm 104:31-33)*

Questions for Discussion

1. Where did you ever experience God? Tell about it!

2. In the Bible, how is the way the writer has God communicate with humankind conditioned by time and culture?

3. How can you be God's co-worker?

5. EVIL AND DEVILS

1. The mystery of evil. In movies and on television shows, the bad guys must be there in order to make it possible for the good guys to prove themselves. But in real life the bad guys are a nuisance. Evil is there, in and around us. It makes life miserable, and we don't know how to eliminate it.

In primitive thinking, disaster, pain, suffering, defeat in war, starvation, and all evils both mental and physical are caused by sin. Therefore, when the writer of Genesis 2 and 3 saw so much evil always and everywhere, he reasoned that there *must* have been sin at the very beginning of the human race. The account of Adam and Eve sinning originated from that trend of thought. However, it offers only a partial answer. Evil is a mystery for which nobody has as yet given an adequate explanation.

2. Our attitude toward evil. Genesis 2 and 3 does not offer us a lesson in a sort of sacred anthropology. We leave it to the scientists to describe how human beings gradually evolved and outgrew the forest. However, the account teaches important lessons: Don't play with temptations! When you have been weak, don't be arrogant or seek to pass the buck. Repent lest God punish you as he punished Adam and Eve in the story.

3. Evil and the devil. Since evil can be so frightening, it is small wonder that less educated people are inclined to personify evil. Think of voodoo cults in our time and country! The primitive people of the Bible saw evil as a person even more than is done today (read Genesis 2 and 3). Hence, healing sickness (caused by sin!) consisted of expelling demons. (See Matthew 8 and 9.)

Does a personal devil exist? We don't know. The Bible mentions evil, but personifying it as a demon/devil is a statement that is conditioned by time and culture and as such does not form part of divine revelation.

The Church regards devils as fallen angels in a permanent state of revolt against God, attempting to lead man to evil. This concept is not clearly stated in the Bible, but is rather the fruit of theological reflection, generally accepted since the time of St. Augustine (4th Century).

4. God helps us overcome evil. Evil remains a mystery and a very tangible reality. But we can overcome evil with the help of Almighty God. Pray Psalm 57 meditatively and apply it to your own life situation. What is your principal weakness? It is the evil that keeps you captive and hinders you from becoming the person your Maker has designed for you to be.

5. Bible reading

Confident prayer for deliverance

Have pity on me, O God; have pity on me,
   for in you I take refuge.
In the shadow of your wings I take refuge,
   till harm pass by.
I call to God the Most High,
   to God, my benefactor.
May he send from heaven and save me;
   may he make those a reproach who trample upon me;
   may God send his kindness and his faithfulness.
I lie prostrate in the midst of lions
   which devour men;
Their teeth are spears and arrows,
   their tongue is a sharp sword.
      Be exalted above the heavens, O God;
      above all the earth be your glory!   *(Psalm 57:2-6)*

Questions for Discussion

1. Discuss how evil is sometimes (but not always) caused by sin. Discuss examples!

2. Why does the Bible make evil a person?

3. What suggestions does the narrative of Genesis 2 and 3 make as to how to cope with evil in and around you?

6. WORD — LIGHT — SON

1. God's communication with human beings. Communication is a complicated thing. It is more than just uttering sounds in English, Chinese, or any other language. Often barriers must first be taken away. Emotions, hard feelings, prejudice, ignorance, and closed-mindedness must be patiently done away with and only then does communication become possible.

What means should God use to communicate with the human race? He is so entirely different from us and so much greater than we are. He is so incomprehensible that we cannot possibly develop an adequate concept of Him!

2. God's Word—Jesus Christ. "In times past, God spoke in fragmentary and varied ways to our fathers through the prophets; in this, the final age, he has spoken to us through his Son" (Hebrews 1:1-2). It is this very core of New Testament literature that John tries to explain in the introduction or prologue to his Gospel version. He uses figures of speech. He calls Jesus God's word to those who are ignorant. He calls Him light to people who walk in darkness.

Jesus of Nazareth, with His charming personality, is God's word to human beings. Prejudice, lack of interest, and closed-mindedness prevent understanding. But could God speak a clearer language than He has done through the appealing personality of Jesus of Nazareth?

3. Jesus—Son of Man. Since Jesus is the most important person of the whole Bible, both Matthew and Luke introduce Him with an impressive genealogy and unusual birth-circumstances. (See Matthew 1–2 and Luke 3:23-38, 1-2.) By working miracles (signs in John!), Jesus revealed His glory. Courageously, He spoke up for the downtrodden, ate with tax collectors and sinners, and irritated the religious power structure of His people which ultimately put Him to death.

But God vindicated Jesus by raising Him up. Inspired by the awareness that Jesus is alive, His followers started the world-wide movement for a better world, called the Kingdom (Reign) of God.

4. Jesus—Son of God. Aware that Jesus is alive, the early followers meditated on who this mysterious man was. Indeed, a prophet—God's spokesman, His word, His light, His Son. But if He is all of this now as exalted with God, He was so also during His lifetime, when He was baptized by John (Matthew 3:13-17), already at His conception and birth (Luke 1:35), and in John's reflection even as pre-existent with the Father (John 1:1-18).

Recapitulating this in final reflection, the Bible views Jesus as so intimately one with God that He is simply called God, with full understanding, however, that He remains man as well (John 10:22-25, 30-39). Meditate on these passages and respond in prayer!

5. Mary—Mother of God. Whether a mother is un-lettered or carries a Ph.D., when her son is a medical doctor she *is* the mother of a medical doctor. If Jesus is not only man but also God, His Mother Mary is indeed the Mother of God.

Hence, all generations of Christians honor Mary as such and pray: "Holy Mary, Mother of God, pray for us sinners." We believe in the communion of saints; both those at this side of the grave and those in the hereafter can pray for one another.

6. Bible reading

Jesus' Divinity

The Word became flesh
and made his dwelling among us,
and we have seen his glory:
The glory of an only Son coming from the Father,
filled with enduring love.
John testified to him by proclaiming: "This is he of whom I said, 'The one who comes after me ranks ahead of me, for he was before me.' "
Of his fullness
we have all had a share—
love following upon love.   *(John 1:14-16)*

Jesus' Mission

Now John in prison heard about the works Christ was per-forming, and sent a message by his disciples to ask him, "Are you 'He who is to come' or do we look for another?" In reply, Jesus said to them: "Go back and report to John what you hear and see: the blind recover their sight, cripples walk, lepers are cured, the deaf hear, dead men are raised to life, and the poor have the good news preached to them."   *(Matthew 11:2-5)*

Jesus' Death

After that, Jesus realizing that everything was now finished, said to fulfill the Scripture, "I am thirsty." There was a jar there, full of common wine. They stuck a sponge soaked in this wine on some hyssop and raised it to his lips. When Jesus took the wine, he said, "Now it is finished." Then he bowed his head, and delivered over his spirit.   *(John 19:28-30)*

Jesus' Resurrection

I handed on to you first of all what I myself received, that Christ died for our sins in accordance with the Scriptures; that he was buried and, in accordance with the Scriptures, rose on the third day; that he was seen by Cephas, then by the Twelve.

In any case, whether it be I or they, this is what we preach and this is what you believed.   *(1 Corinthians 15:3-5, 11)*

Questions for Discussion

1. Read Matthew 1:1-24 and discuss with your instructor how to understand this in referral to Genesis 18:9-15; 21:1-4; Judges 13; 1 Samuel 1:9-23; Luke 1:1-24.

2. Read Matthew 8—9 and discuss with your instructor how to understand all of this.

3. Discuss how in retrospect the theologians of the New Testament came to see Jesus as Son of God and finally as God. (See also Chap. 3,3.)

7.

RECONCILIATION

"That this nation, under God, shall have a new birth of freedom" [Lincoln's Gettysburg Address].

1. Approaches to a mystery. Sometimes, we call a friend a mystery. There is something in him/her that we don't grasp. There is more than we first suspected at face value. A mystery cannot be understood fully. It can be approached, however, by using metaphors and figures of speech which suggest likeness or analogy. Theologians use this method when they try to say something meaningful about the mystery of Christ.

2. Models of sin and reconciliation. We observe the sad reality that all of us have sinned and need reconciliation with God. And we believe that Jesus Christ has something to do with that process of reconciliation. Biblical theologians use reconciliation models such as atonement, sacrifice, ransom, and expiation to describe Jesus' role in the process of our reconciliation with God.

These metaphors were meaningful for Biblical people, since bloody sacrifices were part and parcel of their religious culture. For centuries handbooks of religion have repeated these metaphors verbatim, even though the latter have lost most of their meaning for us who don't offer God bloody sacrifices any more.

3. Jesus—Exemplary cause of salvation. Nowadays, we are invited to find idioms of our own to say something meaningful about our reconciliation with God in Jesus Christ. In doing so, we observe first of all that our sole redeemer is God, and that Jesus as man is only the mediator or executor of our reconciliation. With this in mind, we are encouraged to approach the mystery of our reconciliation in Christ by seeing Jesus firstly as the *exemplary* cause of salvation. This means that in Christ we find illumination and inspiration. (See Chap. 6, 3 and 4.)

We see Jesus with His life of total dedication, terminated by a violent death but vindicated in the resurrection, as an exemplar. We are able to live a fully human and meaningful life by doing as He did, i.e., dedicating ourselves to real values and knowing in faith that we will live forever. Jesus is the first fruits. We follow!

4. Jesus—making intercession. Besides being an exemplar (see no. 3, above), Jesus' life of dedication and obedience, which resulted in a cruel death, was also one continuous prayer. And as fully alive Jesus still intercedes for us. We believe in the communion of saints, i.e., all the saints, both in this life and in the hereafter, can meaningfully pray for one another.

Hence, with greater reason will God take redemptive initiatives because of our Lord's prayer for all humankind. And since "offering sacrifice" is just another form of praying, the metaphor of sacrifice as causing our redemption is meaningful. We will discuss this more extensively in Chapter 14 on the Eucharistic Celebration.

Read the Bible passages and thank God for Jesus Who made possible your redemption from evil and your reconciliation with Him. If you get lost, ask your instructor to help you. Apply the lesson to your own life situation and respond in prayer.

5. Relevance of Biblical metaphors. Does this mean that the reconciliation metaphors of the Bible (atonement, sacrifice, ransom, expiation) are all of a sudden meaningless? Not at all ! The cruel deaths of the civil rights workers of the sixties had a redeeming and healing effect on our bigoted society. Seemingly, they were necessary to bring many to realize how evil social injustice is and consequently lead to conversions.

In a similar vein, we may see Jesus as exemplary cause of our redemption. His life of dedication to the Kingdom and His courageous speaking up for the down-trodden, which resulted in His cruel death, make us acknowledge how evil sin (aversion from God) is. Indeed, "by his stripes we are healed" (Isaiah 53:5).

6. Uniqueness of Jesus. Was Jesus then just another "civil rights worker" and not unique as taught by the Church? Jesus is unique because His liberation movement is not merely political. Rather it is an ongoing process in the hearts of all people of all times and it includes God and a happy hereafter. The unique and universal meaning of Jesus and His mission was clearly emphasized by God when He vindicated Jesus, His life and death, by raising Him from the dead.

Discuss the article of the Creed, "He descended into hell," meaning sheol (in Hebrew thinking, "the pit") not gehenna, which would mean hell properly speaking. To descend into sheol signifies "to really die." Refer to 1 Peter 3:18-22 and 4:6. Jesus is the future of those who no longer have a future. (See p. 16.)

7. Bible reading

Our eyes fixed on Jesus

Therefore, since we for our part are surrounded by this cloud of witnesses, let us lay aside every encumbrance of sin which clings to us and persevere in running the race which lies ahead; let us keep our eyes fixed on Jesus, who inspires and perfects our faith. For the sake of the joy which lay before him he endured the cross, heedless of its shame. He has taken his seat at the right of the throne of God. Remember how he endured the opposition of sinners; hence do not grow despondent or abandon the struggle. In your fight against sin you have not yet resisted to the point of shedding blood.   *(Hebrews 12:1-4)*

Forever making intercession

Under the old covenant there were many priests because they were prevented by death from remaining in office; but Jesus, because he remains forever, has a priesthood which does not pass away. Therefore he is always able to save those who approach God through him, since he forever lives to make intercession for them. It was fitting that we should have such a high priest: holy, innocent, undefiled, separated from sinners, higher than the heavens. Unlike the other high priest, he has no need to offer sacrifice day after day, first for his own sins and then for those of the people; he did that once for all when he offered himself.   *(Hebrews 7:23-27)*

Questions for Discussion

1. What concepts do Biblical theologians use to approach our reconciliation with God in and through Jesus Christ?
2. Which two approaches to the mystery of our reconciliation through Christ are suggested for our time?
3. How is Jesus unique?

8. THE BREATH OF YAHWEH

1. Manifestation of personal presence. You are locally present to people surrounding you in an over-crowded bus or subway. But that is not a personal presence. A person is personally present to you only if there is a mutual disclosure of self. This is the presence of friends and lovers. The more there is an openness of mind and heart, the more two persons are present to one another.

This should be the presence of God's Spirit in you. The more you are open to the Spirit and establish a dialogue of love in prayer, the more He is present to you.

2. Manifestation of personal presence. Ever since the "ruah-Yahweh," the spirit (breath) of God, hovered over the water, like an eagle hovering over its young (Genesis 1:2; Deuteronomy 32:11), God was seen as giving and protecting life. The symbols used to describe the life-giving Spirit of God are breath, fire, tongues, and a strong driving wind. The fire of the Holy Spirit enlightened the hearts of Jesus' disciples and gave them the courage and strength to preach the Gospel to all nations.

The background of Luke's narrative (see Acts 2:1-11 below!) may have been a charismatic prayer meeting. "Speaking in tongues," as is done nowadays again in prayer groups, is a very early phenomenon. Read 1 Corinthians 12:1-11 and 14! New languages (tongues!), prophecies, and ecstasies may accompany the outpouring of the Spirit. But don't forget that every gift of God receives its shape from the environment in which it is poured out.

Religious custom, character, and culture have something to do with the way in which the Spirit manifests Himself. John 20:19-23 (below!) mentions a more quiet and less emotional communication of God's Spirit. Seemingly there is room for both. However, God's Spirit should be a moving force in you.

3. Transformation in the Spirit. Often great men, who accomplished marvelous things in their lives, have admitted that they owed a great deal to the inspiring presence of their wives. The relationship to their wives was a dynamic force that transformed them, making them to a certain degree different persons. In a similar vein, we may see God's gracious presence to us, His self-communication, giving us His spirit. It transforms us as all relationships do. (See chap. 1,1.) The Bible calls this transformation rebirth from water and the Spirit (John 3:1-4)—"born again!"

4. God as Trinity and as Love. Relating the mystery of His self-communication to all of us, the Bible mentions *the Father* (as originator of all life, related to creation), sending *His Son or Word* (for our salvation) and communicating *the Spirit* (related to our rebirth.) These are meaningful metaphors, telling us first of all what God means for us, and then to a certain extent also about

God Himself. Theological reflection later speaks of the Blessed Trinity, three persons in one God.

You may discuss with your instructor how contemporary theologians approach this mystery, and why they do it in a different way (as three modes of being in God). But keep in mind that more important than knowing *about* God is knowing God as *"Love."* You know your beloved and she/he knows you. It is that kind of knowledge which ultimately satisfies a human being. Read meditatively Romans 11:33-36 (below), mark what touched your heart and respond prayerfully!

5. Bible reading

Promise of the Spirit

On one occasion when he met with them, he told them not to leave Jerusalem: "Wait, rather, for the fulfillment of my Father's promise, of which you have heard me speak. John baptized with water, but within a few days you will be baptized with water, but within a few days you will be baptized with the holy Spirit." *(Acts 1:4-5)*

Descent of the Spirit

When the day of Pentecost came it found them gathered in one place. Suddenly from up in the sky there came a noise like a strong, driving wind which was heard all through the house where they were seated. Tongues as of fire appeared, which parted and came to rest on each of them. All were filled with the Holy Spirit. They began to express themselves in foreign tongues and make bold proclamation as the Spirit prompted them.

Staying in Jerusalem at the time were devout Jews of every nation under heaven. These heard the sound, and assembled in a large crowd. They were much confused because each one heard these men speaking his own language. The whole occurrence astonished them. They asked in utter amazement, "Are not all of these men who are speaking Galileans? How is it that each of us hears them in his native tongue? We are Parthians, Medes, and Elamites. We live in Mesopotamia, Judea and Cappadocia, Pontus, the province of Asia, Phrygia and Pamphylia,

Egypt, and the regions of Libya around Cyrene. There are even visitors from Rome—all Jews, or those who have come over to Judaism; Cretans and Arabs too. Yet each of us hears them speaking in his own tongue about the marvels God has accomplished." *(Acts 2:1-11)*

Reception of the Spirit

On the evening of that first day of the week, even though the disciples had locked the doors of the place where they were for fear of the Jews, Jesus came and stood before them. "Peace be with you," he said. When he had said this, he showed them his hands and his side. At the sight of the Lord the disciples rejoiced. "Peace be with you," he said again.

"As the Father has sent me,
so I send you."
Then he breathed on them and said:
"Receive the Holy Spirit.
If you forgive men's sins,
they are forgiven them;
if you hold them bound,
they are held bound." *(John 20:19-23)*

The Unfathomable mystery of God

How deep are the riches and wisdom and the knowledge of God! How inscrutable his judgments, how unsearchable his ways! For "who has known the mind of the Lord? Or who has been his counselor? Who has given him anything so as to deserve return?" For from him and through him and for him all things are. To him be glory forever. Amen. *(Romans 11:33-36)*

Questions for Discussion

1. Using the Biblical metaphors breath, fire, tongues, and wind, discuss what God's Spirit should do to you.
2. What has relationship to do with rebirth from water and the Spirit?
3. Why is knowing God more important than knowing about God?

9. PEOPLE, KING, SHEEP AND SHEPHERD

1. Togetherness. There are very few things, we are able to do alone. "Birds of a feather flock together." Both organized crime and organized religion follow the same instinct. We do things together. Whether it is a ladies' garden club, the CYO or the Shriners, there is no fun in doing it alone, and "alone" it does not last.

2. Christianity to be lived in groups. Constantly living up to the beautiful ideals of Christianity (defeating evil in and around us—loving God and neighbor as ourselves) must be done together. We need one another's inspiration. Going back into history, we see that both our Lord and His early disciples knew this. They clearly designed their program for a better world (God's kingdom!) to be lived not alone but in groups or congregations.

3. God's people. Paradigms (models) were borrowed from the Hebrew Bible to bring out this idea of togetherness. One of them is the legendary kingdom of David. He united the scattered tribes of Israel into one fierce and free kingdom. Over the centuries ever more idealized in literature, King David became the model of Hebrew greatness and pride. He was truly a son of God, God's representative to the people as sung in the inauguration hymn: "The Lord /Yahweh/ said to my Lord /my master, king David/: 'Sit at my right hand /share power with me/.'" Read and discuss with your instructor Psalm 110 below.

In this vein, the writers of the New Testament describe the Christian movement as a Kingdom with Jesus as a Davidic king. We, the Church, are God's people with Jesus, His Son, His representative, to rule and guide us. And consequently Psalm 110 was applied to Jesus.

4. Becoming a real part of God's people. Another paradigm is the Davidic king as shepherd. In Biblical times, sheep, goats, and shepherds were part and parcel of daily life. The Lord said to David: "You shall shepherd my people Israel" (2 Samuel 5:2). The author of John's Gospel expatiates on this theme extensively. (See John 10, 11-15 below!)

Since we are no longer familiar with sheep and shepherds, we can translate this bucolic "shepherd-flock" model into the paradigms "family of believers" and "community of disciples" (Acts 6:2), which have more appeal for believers of our culture. Many young people turn to gurus who came from the East. Discipleship implies a process of ongoing learning from the guru and often living with him in a commune. And that is our situation as related to the Maha Guru (Supreme Teacher) Jesus Christ.

In this setting, Mary could be seen as prototype of *believer*-disciple and Peter as prototype of *apostle*-disciple. Some of both should constantly grow in us. And a sense of solidarity, kept alive by affective relationships with mature and exemplary Christians, is mandatory.

You may ask: "What do I do to contribute to a greater togetherness in my parish? Is my parish a real church-home with an atmosphere of belonging for all? What can I or the parish council do about it?" Attend the meetings of the parish council and let your voice be heard! Criticizing others is easy. A parish cannot be a sign of God's Kingdom (Reign) to a community if members attend Mass on Sunday and then hurry somewhere else.

5. Bible Reading

The Messiah: King, Priest and Conqueror

The Lord said to my Lord: "Sit at my right hand
   till I make your enemies your footstool."
The scepter of your power the Lord will stretch forth from
      Zion:
   "Rule in the midst of your enemies.
Yours is princely power in the day of your birth, in holy splendor;
   before the daystar, like the dew, I have begotten you."
The Lord has sworn, and he will not repent:
   "You are a priest forever, according to the order of Melchizedek."
The Lord is at your right hand;
   he will crush kings on the day of his wrath.   *(Psalm 110)*

(Psalm 110)

Jesus the Good Shepherd

I am the good shepherd;
the good shepherd lays down his life for the sheep.
The hired hand—who is no shepherd
nor owner of the sheep—
catches sight of the wolf coming
and runs away, leaving the sheep
to be snatched and scattered by the wolf.
That is because he works for pay;
he has no concern for the sheep.

I am the good shepherd.
I know my sheep
and my sheep know me
in the same way that the Father knows me
and I know the Father;
for these sheep I will give my life.   *(John 10:11-15)*

Questions for Discussion

1. Discuss the need of doing things together by mentioning examples and applying them to Church life.

2. Discuss the paradigms mentioned in this chapter and how they apply to the Church today, which is no longer familiar with kings, sheep, and shepherds. What can we learn from gurus who came from the East? Discuss some of them. In what do we disagree with them?

3. Discuss Psalm 110 together. How does it apply to you?

"He who lives in me and I in him, will produce abundantly" *(John 15:5)*.

10. RELATED TO THE FOUNDER

1. Return to American origins. In high school, we had to learn about the founding fathers of our nation and their vision of an ideal society, in which there would be no room for the deficiencies that plagued the old country and made most settlers cross the ocean to build up a new future in this land of the free. Time and again each generation of Americans must turn to the original documents and draw inspiration from them to remain faithful to the ideals which made this country great.

2. Return to Christian origins. The founding father of the Christian movement (the Kingdom of God on earth) is Jesus Christ. He had a vision of an ideal society, in which there would be no room for the legalism that plagued the Jewish community of His day. He came to set us free from having to observe laws just for law's sake. Human beings should be free; they must not, however, abuse their freedom but use it for love.

Time and again, we who are Jesus' followers should turn to the ancient documents (New Testament!), which tell us about Jesus' dreams and aspirations. They should inspire us to forward His ideas and keep on establishing God's Reign on earth

3. Intimate relationship with Jesus. As Americans, we relate to George Washington. As Christians, we relate to Jesus Christ. In the Bible, we have two well-known metaphors which describe our relationship with the Lord Jesus, namely, "the Vine and the Branches" and "the many Members in one Body." In the previous chapter, we discussed the Church, you and me, as God's people and Jesus' flock, a community of disciples.

The comparison of the vine and the branches indicates an intimate person-to-person relationship with our living Lord. Relationships made you whatever you are as a person (see chap. 1,1) and you must keep them alive in order not to deteriorate and become a peculiar loner. Prayerful Bible reading is a must to keep growing in intimacy with our Lord.

4. Integrative function of Jesus in the Church. As for the many members in one body, we know that a body is made up of related parts. What keeps those parts together and makes them function properly? Our brain does this job, although we know very little about how it is done. In addition to many specific functions (imagining, reasoning, remembering), the brain has an integrative function. It is the organ which unifies the body and integrates the activity of all the organs. When this integrative function of the brain is lost, the body is no longer a living organism but a collection of dying organs, tissues, and cells, which soon fall apart.

Jesus has an integrative function with relation to His body, the Church. Losing contact with Him means falling apart like dying tissues and cells.

5. Function of Church leaders. The comparison tells us also that not all members of the Church have the same function. Each contributes to the parish according to ability. The coordinator is the pastor. Jesus' Spirit has been given to all members, but to our leaders in a special way. That is why, as a rule, we follow. While attentively listening to the Spirit's movement everywhere, our leaders give guidelines.

However, priests, bishops, and the Holy Father (as Bishop of Rome, head of the bishops!) do not exercise authority as is often done in secular society. Their leadership is characterized not by power but by brotherly service, as Jesus has told us. Besides the Scriptures below, meditatively read also 1 Corinthians 12:12-31. Mark whatever applies to you and respond in prayer. For ministry in the Church, see also Chap. 18.

6. Bible reading

Life in Jesus

Live on in me, as I do in you.
No more than a branch can bear fruit of itself
apart from the vine,
can you bear fruit
apart from me.
I am the vine, you are the branches.
He who lives in me and I in him,
will produce abundantly,
for apart from me you can do nothing.
A man who does not live in me
is like a withered, rejected branch,
picked up to be thrown in the fire and burnt.
If you live in me,
and my words stay part of you
you may ask what you will—
it will be done for you.

(John 15:4-7)

Jesus—Support of the Body

Rather, let us profess the truth in love and grow to the full maturity of Christ the head. Through him the whole body grows, and with the proper functioning of the members joined firmly together by each supporting ligament, builds itself up in love. *(Romans 12:4-5)*

One Body in Christ

Just as each of us has one body with many members, and not all the members have the same function, so too we, though many, are one body in Christ and individually members one of another. *(Ephesians 4:15-16)*

Questions for Discussion

1. For every movement or organization, why is it important to relate constantly to the founder(s)? Discuss examples and apply to the Church!

2. Discuss how recent changes in the Church may relate to the necessity discussed under 1.

3. Discuss the function of Jesus' Spirit and authority in the Church.

After Vatican II, ecumenical gatherings with people of other religious persuasions have become common in the Church.

11. GROPING FOR TRUTH

1. Limited knowledge of religious realities. From your high school days you may be familiar with John Godfrey Saxe's didactic poem "The Blind Men and the Elephant." Six blind men want to see the elephant, but they must do so by just touching him. One feels his tusk and thinks the elephant is a spear. Another feels the knee and thinks the elephant is a tree. Still another seizes the tail and says: "I see, the elephant is very like a rope." All six men get their own partial insight.

Whatever the aesthetic value of the poem, it brings out that we can know "The Unseen Beyond" only partially. The mysteries of the Faith cannot be fully understood and explained. They can only be approached with the very limited means available to human beings.

2. Limited understanding of revealed truths. We Christians in the Catholic tradition are grateful for the fullness of Divine revelation, received in Jesus Christ, but we are also aware that we don't have all the answers that the modern mind is seeking. Although God has revealed Himself as a loving Father, we realize that "Father" is just another metaphor, albeit a very prefrecious one, which tells us something about God. We don't have an adequate concept of who God is. We observe the same limitation concerning the mystery of suffering, the how of life hereafter, and existence as such.

The Bible indicates a few facts, but does not offer an adequate explanation. The Church teaches, but we know that neither Pope nor Bishops have a hotline to the Holy Spirit. They are leading men in the community (Acts 15:22), and we believe that the Spirit has been given to them in a special way, but they must grope prayerfully for truth just as all of us, guided by God's Spirit, do. (See Chap. 10,5.)

3. Partial truth found everywhere. We are committed to our Faith, take it as definite, and believe that in Christ there is fullness of truth, yet also aware that we never fully comprehend this truth. The Second Vatican Council states that truth, though partial, is found everywhere. Hence, we dialogue with all people, who seriously search with us. Non-Christian religions also contain enrichment, if only we are ready to discover it in patient and honest dialogue. And a Chinese in central China who has never heard of Christ but is an honest person, i.e., acts according to what his conscience dictates as good, will be saved.

Following this insight, we still admire St. Francis Xavier and thousands of dedicated missionaries of the past, although we can no longer agree with their methods of convert-making. By both word and example, modern missionaries , you and I, show the beauty of a Christian life-style. They are present in any community like yeast in dough, and as such they try to have an elevating impact, challenging all around them to be better people in their own faith. And when they encounter the desire for futher information, they will offer it.

4. A divided Church. With larger communities (Eastern Orthodox — Anglican — Protestant Churches) separated from full communion with the Catholic Church, we are not the Church as Christ wants her to be. A divided Church is sinful. It does not make sense to blame one another for these divisions. All of us are guilty.

We are a "pilgrim Church," sinful by our divisions, but moving toward a new oneness in Christ. We pray that the so-called Ecumenical Movement may result in that oneness which Christ prayed for so ardently.

5. Bible reading

Preach the Word

You have followed closely my teaching and my conduct. . . . You know what persecutions I have had to bear, and you know how the Lord saved me from them all. Anyone who wants to live a godly life in Christ Jesus can expect to be persecuted. But all the while evil men and charlatans will go from bad to worse, deceiving others, themselves deceived. You, for your part, must remain faithful to what you have learned and believed, because you know who your teachers were. Likewise, from your infancy you have known the sacred Scriptures, the source of the wisdom which through faith in Jesus Christ leads to salvation. All Scripture is inspired of God and useful for teaching—for reproof, correction, and training in holiness so that the man of God may be fully competent and equipped for every good work.

I charge you to preach the word, to stay with this task whether convenient or inconvenient—correcting, reproving, appealing—constantly teaching and never losing patience.

(2 Timothy 3:10-17; 4:2)

Questions for Discussion

1. We often hear: "We are the greatest!" May we apply this statement to the Catholic Church? Why or why not?

2. Discuss the Ecumenical Movement with your instructor.

3. All of us should be missionaries! Discuss the old and new way of convert-making

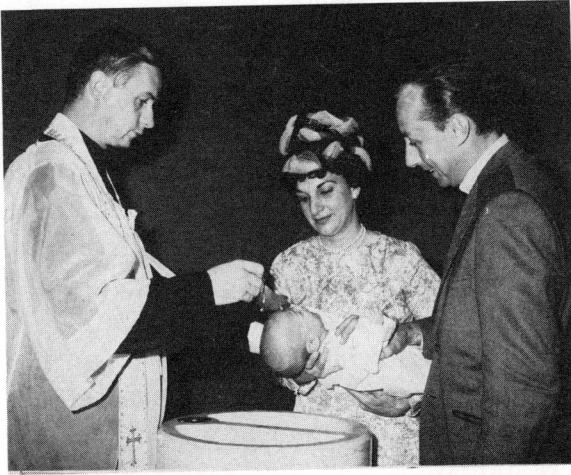

12. CHRISTIAN INITIATION

1. Secular rites of initiation. A great landmark for the Africans comes during adolescence when they undergo formal initiation (incorporation) into adulthood and the mysteries of the tribe. The "rites of passage" (passing from adolescence into adulthood) consists of tortuous ceremonies such as circumcision and knocking out or pulling one or more teeth. Initiation strengthens the vital forces received from the ancestors and makes the candidates aware of their status as man and woman, fully responsible for their duties in the clan (extended family).

In our culture, we have the initiation into the mysteries of the Shriners, Knights of Columbus/Peter Claver, sororities and fraternities. Some of these initiations, too, are fairly rigorous, and the whole ceremony must be kept secret. The candidates have to prove themselves and accept the responsibilities of their membership.

2. Total union with Christ. In the early Church, when candidates were initiated into the mysteries of the Christian Faith, they were totally immersed in a bath of water. Symbolically they died with Christ, i.e., they died to their old sinful selves, in order to rise up out of the water as new creatures, fully alive with the risen Lord.

They were born again from water and the Holy Spirit, Who henceforth dwelled in them as a life-giving force. Sharing fellowship with the risen Lord in the symbolism of bread and wine (Eucharist—The Lord's Supper) was the second stage of the celebration. Accepting full responsibility in their new family of believers was tied in with it.

3. Changes in the rites. In later ages, we see changes in those "rites of passage" (passing from your old selfish Ego into a new loving person), which were not always for the better. During the fifth century, infant Baptism replaced the adult initiation. Actually, the initiation was stretched out over a number of years:

a. Baptism at infancy (by pouring water over the head of the candidate, although immersion is allowed);

b. the Eucharist at the age of reason or discernment;

c. the final touch when the young persons are able to make their own profession of faith. This final touch, done by the bishop himself, became known later as "Confirmation."

Only when an adult is initiated is everything done in one ceremony or series of symbolical acts. Bathing with water, seen as life-giving (rain on the grass after a long period of drought!), remains the main symbolism, although it is no longer as suggestive as when the candidate was totally immersed and came out of the water as a new creature!

4. Religious meaning of the rite. It is important to understand the creative language of the ritual, the effective and penetrating Word, underlined by meaningful symbolism. It is a word praying for the candidate, who is going to be bathed in light and supported by the care of parents, friends, and relatives.

There is prayer for strength, underlined by anointing. There is reference to the Spirit, Who breathed on tne waters at the dawn of creation, as well as to the waters of the Flood which made an end of sin and a new beginning of goodness, the waters of the Red Sea through which Israel marched into freedom, and the waters of the Jordan in which Jesus was baptized. All of this solicits the candidate's affirmation of faith, without which the required encounter with God does not take place.

Then there was/is the immersion into water or bathing with water, which stands for dying with Christ to your old sinful self and rising up with Him as a new creature. It is done in the name of the Father, Son, and Holy Spirit. Another anointing symbolizes your royal and priestly dignity as a Christian.

You are clothed in Christ—a clean garment as symbol! And you receive a candle, lighted from the Paschal candle, the Light of Christ, the Faith, which must be kept burning and alive. The imposition of hands stands for communicating the Sacred, the Holy Spirit as a seal, symbolized by another anointing (Confirmation). Celebrating the event by sharing table fellowship with the risen Lord Jesus and fellow Christians completes the Initiation into the mysteries of God's people, of which you are an adult member, fully responsible for its well-being.

5. Bible reading

Death to sin, life in God

What, then, are we to say? "Let us continue in sin that grace may abound"? Certainly not! How can we who died to sin go on living in it? Are you not aware that we who are baptized into Christ Jesus were baptized into his death? Through baptism into his death we were buried with him, so that, just as Christ was raised from the dead by the glory of the Father, we too might live a new life. If we have been united with him through likeness to his death, so shall we be through a like resurrection.

(Romans 6:1-5)

Clothed with Christ

Each one of you is a son of God because of your faith in Christ Jesus. All of you who have been baptized into Christ have clothed yourselves with him. There does not exist among you Jew or Greek, slave or freeman, male or female. All are one in Christ Jesus. Furthermore, if you belong to Christ you are the descendants of Abraham, which means you inherit all that was promised.

(Galatians 3:26-29)

Questions for Discussion

1. Going through the Rite of Christian Initiation, explain the symbolic use of water for Baptism.
2. What does the imposition of hands stand for?
3. Why is the candidate's affirmation of Faith essential in the rite of initiation?

13. INTIMACY — AFFIRMATION

1. Need for intimacy and affirmation. A serious ailment in our day is alienation. It ruins marriages, populates jails, and keeps the waiting rooms of mental health clinics filled with people who desperately search for intimacy and affirmation. In order to be happy and function normally we need both. This need for intimacy and affirmation prompts the human beings to marry. "It is not good for the man to be alone" (Genesis 1:18).

Nevertheless, in the Catholic tradition, we observe that quite a few people choose the celibate life-style. Our priests, sisters, and religious brothers go through life without that "suitable partner" mentioned by the Bible (Genesis 1:18). Can they do without intimacy and affirmation?

2. Intimate relationship with God. All of us, married and not married, need intimacy and affirmation, although the celibate searches for it without getting involved sexually. All life is relationship (see Chap. 1,1). Celibates develop human relations, as all of us should do. Moreover, all of us should develop an intimate relationship with God, in Whom we live and move and have our being (Acts 17:28). He is love, and if you abide in love, you abide in God and God in you (1 John 4:16).

This is an intimate relationship, which is not even possible between spouses. Indeed, lovers relate to one another intimately, but there remains always the wall of individuality. Lovers remain two distinct individuals, and ultimately each must go it alone. This is not so between me and my Maker, Who wants to be my spouse (Isaiah 54:5). There is no wall of individuality. To a certain extent, I am God.

Hindu theologians speak of "advaita." Christian theologians call it "non-duality." Since I am intimately related to God, I never have to feel alone, abandoned, or rejected. He made me; hence I am precious in His eyes, regardless of what people think of me.

3. Vowed celibacy. Is this degree of intimacy the prerogative of celibates only? No! All can and should enjoy it. (see Chap. 19,3.) Vowed celibacy creates a special relationship with God. As such it results in a special life-style for those who feel called to it. But intimacy with God is not the exclusive privilege of celibates.

4. Intimacy kept alive by communication. How can we keep this intimacy with God—that feeling of being affirmed by Him—alive and exciting? As in the case of all relationships, the answer is by communication. Lack of communication causes alienation, which makes marriage and friendship boring and finally terminates them. Communication with God is called prayer, meditation, or contemplation. When you neglect it, you drift apart from God. Divorcees usually blame one another. When you get divorced from your Spouse, Who is your Maker (Isaiah 54:5), blame only yourself!

5. Value of meditation. For centuries, Catholics have reserved meditation for priests and religious. Lay people were supposed to say the rosary, recite litanies and prayers, which others had made up for them. Of course, there is nothing wrong with this kind of prayer, and when we pray together in church, we must use formulas as an alternative for chaos. (See pp. 95 and 99.) But we should learn to meditate, especially from the Bible, God's word to us.

Biblical meditations are discursive (through images, forms and figures). Only gradually, can you pass on to the state of contemplation, being grasped by the loving awareness of God without the acts of intellect, memory and will. Ask your instructor for guidance! You might also begin with the meditations found in my book: "Bible Meditations for Every Day."

6. Bible reading

God's Everlasting Love

For he who has become your husband is your Maker;
   his name is the Lord of hosts;
Your redeemer is the Holy One of Israel,
   called God of all the earth.
The Lord calls you back,
   like a wife forsaken and grieved in spirit ...
Though the mountains leave their place
   and the hills be shaken,
My love shall never leave you
   nor my covenant of peace be shaken,
   says the Lord, who has mercy on you.   *(Isaiah 54:5-6, 9-10)*

Questions for Discussion

1. Discuss cases of alienation, their apparent reasons and sad results.

2. Discuss the celibate life-style and its motivations.

3. What is "non-duality" and how can we keep intimacy with God exciting?

14. THE EUCHARISTIC CELEBRATION

1. Showing love by giving. Christmas, Valentine's Day, birthdays, and anniversaries are the beloved times for showing love and affection by giving. If you should forget, the business people both on television and in your local mall will remind you. Flowers, or any kind of gift, are apt tokens of self-giving in love and appreciation. And at a farewell party for a retiring employee, the words of thanks and appreciation are usually under-lined, emphasized, and summed up by offering a gift!

Ever since the dawn of humankind, people have tried to please the gods, and God, *by giving*. A gift to God is usually called a *sacrifice*. In time of disaster, which in the mind of primitive people was always caused by sin, they offered *sin-offerings* for atonement. An angry God had to be placated. When a sacrificial lamb was burnt up, it was called a *holocaust* with its symbolism focused on the fragrant smoke going up to God. When in honor of a deity, blood or wine was poured on the ground, the altar, or a victim, it was called a *libation*. Actually, offering sacrifice to God is another form of praying, just as giving a present is a particular way of saying "Thank you. I appreciate it!"

2. Use of reconciliation concepts. The theologians of the New Testament, especially the writers of Hebrews and 1 Peter, often use the reconciliation concepts: sacrifice, sin-offering, holocaust, libation, as metaphors to approach the mystery of Jesus' life, death, and resurrection which reconciled the sinful human race with God. Attributing sacrificial connotations to the Lord's suffering and death was very meaningful for people of their time and culture, since they were familiar with bloody sacrifices and sin-offerings. (See chapter 7: "Reconciliation.")

3. Sacrificial connotations. When gradually the theology of Hebrews and 1 Peter dominated other theologies of the New Testament, metaphorically God's people was seen ever more as a priestly people. Moreover, sacrificial connotations were given to the Eucharist—The Lord's Supper. In the bread and the wine, signifying the Lord's body and blood, His sacrifice of Calvary was seen present, and God's priestly people was invited to make it a token of self-giving to God in thanksgiving.

4. Eucharist as sacrifice and table fellowship. Ever since, in the Roman Catholic tradition, the Eucharist is seen as both sacrifice and table fellowship with our Lord and one another. All four of the Eucharistic Prayers authorized for use in this country emphasize a sacrificial connotation and so do other prayers of the Roman Mass. Our brothers and sisters of the Reformation emphasize more the meal connotation.

5. Emphasis on aspect of self-giving. Since we are no longer familiar with bloody sacrifices, sin-offerings, holocausts, and libations, such concepts mean very little to us today. Happily, we are still familiar with giving presents as tokens of our self-giving, as signs of thanksgiving, appreciation, and even as a token of saying: "I'm sorry" (atonement). It is in this vein that we should see our participation in the Eucharist.

We can forget about any "bloody" or "burning up" connotations and concentrate on the symbolism of self-giving to God in and through our Lord's giving of self during His life and cruel death. Read the four Eucharistic Prayers. Words are spoken and a gift—bread and wine, the Body and Blood of Christ—signifies whatever has been said. (See no. 1, above.) Make it a token of your self-giving to God. "May He /Christ/ make us an everlasting gift to You /God the Father/" (Prayer III).

You might begin using the "St. Joseph Sunday Missal," for which I wrote the themes and Biblical commentaries. These may help you to understand the Sunday Liturgy better. Ask your instructor how to use the Missal.

6. Bible reading
Christ, the perfect priest

It was fitting that we should have such a high priest: holy, innocent, undefiled, separated from sinners, higher than the heavens. Unlike the other high priest, he has no need to offer sacrifice day after day, first for his own sins and then for those of the people; he did that once for all when he offered himself. For the law sets up as high priest men who are weak, but the word of the oath which came after the law appoints as priest the Son, made perfect forever.   *(Hebrew 7:26-28)*

Questions for Discussion

1. Why do the writers of the New Testament time and again use Old Testament metaphors of reconciliation to approach Jesus' involvement in our reconciliation with God? Discuss some of them!

2. As regards the Lord's Supper, what happened when the theology of Hebrews and 1 Peter took over in significance?

3. How should you participate in the Eucharist?

15. TABLE FELLOWSHIP

1. Table fellowship means people. We see a profound difference between a turkey dinner eaten in a restaurant by a lonesome traveler and a similar dinner enjoyed by parents, children, and grandchildren, who have come from a distance to celebrate Thanksgiving at home. Diplomats may come to this country for delicate discussions, but a state dinner seems to belong to such visits. And we go to a party not just for punch, highballs and snacks, but for people.

Our Lord enjoyed table fellowship very much. He was not an austere prophet like John the Baptizer who lived in the desert and ate only grasshoppers and wild honey (Matthew 3:4). Some even misunderstood our Lord's motivation, and called Him a glutton and drunkard (Matthew 11:18-19). And the last dinner party our Lord had with His disciples was so well remembered that at His wish we still re-enact it time and again "in memory of Him" (Luke 22:19).

Actually, the Liturgy of the Eucharist follows the structure of a Jewish Passover meal. Jesus took the bread, said the Blessing (i.e., the *Berakah*, praising God for what He has done for us), broke it and gave it to His disciples. These four actions—taking, saying the Blessing, breaking, giving—correspond to the Presentation of the gifts, the Eucharistic Prayer (Christian *Berakah*), the

57

breaking of the bread, and Communion. You might check this in your Missal or Missalette.

2. Accepting Christ and others. We have mentioned that in the Roman Catholic tradition, the Eucharist has both a sacrificial and a table fellowship connotation. We are invited to eat the Lord's body, to drink His blood and even to eat His flesh (John 6:51-58). In doing so, we should see no cannibalistic connotations. "Eating my flesh—drinking my blood" is just another Hebrew idiom for "accept me!"

This is precisely what we do at Holy Communion. We accept the Lord Jesus. Symbolically, we celebrate table fellowship with Him, the host, and—as should be done at all parties—not just with the host but with all the fellow guests.

3. Only reality! If you want to be honest, symbolize only reality! To do otherwise is fake, void, meaningless, and, if done consciously, hypocritical. (See 1 Corinthians 11:17-22 below!) Likewise, symbolizing self-surrender to God in and through the Lord's sacrifice, called forth in the symbols of bread and wine, but not living up to your commitment, may direct to you the words Isaiah put figuratively into the mouth of God: see Isaiah 1:11-16 below! Read these Bible passages meditatively, apply them to your own situation, and respond in prayer.

4. Bible reading
The Lord's Supper

What I now have to say is not said in praise, because your meetings are not profitable but harmful. First of all, I hear that when you gather for a meeting there are divisions among you, and I am inclined to believe it. There may even have to be factions among you for the tried and true to stand out clearly. When you assemble it is not to eat the Lord's Supper, for everyone is in haste to eat his own supper. One person goes hungry while another gets drunk. Do you not have homes where you can eat and drink? Would you show contempt for the church of God, and embarrass those who have nothing? What can I say to you? Shall I praise you? Certainly not in this matter!

(1 Corinthians 11:17-22)

God's attitude toward sacrifices

What care I for the number of your sacrifices?
  says the Lord.
I have had enough of whole-burnt rams
  and fat of fatlings;
In the blood of calves, lambs and goats
  I find no pleasure.
When you come in to visit me,
  who asks these things of you?
Trample my courts no more!
  Bring no more worthless offerings;
  your incense is loathsome to me.
New moon and sabbath, calling of assemblies,
  octaves with wickedness: these I cannot bear.
Your new moons and festivals I detest;
  they weigh me down, I tire of the load.
When you spread out your hands,
  I close my eyes to you;
Though you pray the more,
  I will not listen.
Your hands are full of blood!
  Wash yourselves clean!
Put away your misdeeds from before my eyes;
  cease doing evil.   *(Isaiah 1:11-16)*

Questions for Discussion

1. In the perspective of table fellowship, how do you understand "eating the Lord's body/flesh and drinking His blood"?

2. How are you to symbolize reality when you partake in the Lord's supper?

3. Read and discuss Luke 24:13-35 on recognizing the Lord in both Scripture and the breaking of the bread.

16.
SHARING
GUILT

1. Projecting guilt on others. Seemingly, it is difficult to apologize and admit that we have made a mistake, the more so when that mistake was a stupid one or one which involves punishment. Teachers are acquainted with students who bluntly state: "Not me, he did it!" Pride and face-saving results in "projection."

You are acquainted with the Adam and Eve story. Why did a loving God not forgive them? Simply because neither of the two showed the slightest sign of sorrow. The man said: "Not me, but the woman," and the woman said: "Not me, but the snake!" The writer of this story was a keen observer of human life.

2. Serious sin—injury to personal love. Infected by the mystery of evil in and around us—lack of love and honesty, pride, or call it what you will—we are constantly in need of conversion. As a Christian, you have accepted the invitation to an intimate relationship of love with God. However, maturity in love is rare. Evil clouds our vision. Hence, it is not always easy to be faithful to your fundamental option for love.

Nevertheless, keep in mind, that the malignancy of serious sin does not consist in trespassing impersonal laws on the books, as, for example, running through a red traffic light. It consists in the injury to personal love, the love of God and fellow human beings. You break up a relationship.

3. Apology and forgiveness. When aware of guilt, can you apologize and forgive on the human level? If not, stop praying: "And forgive us...as we forgive those who trespass [sin] against us!" The Bible is not interested merely in repentance for and reparation of each individual transgression of the Divine law, but in a new attitude. "A clean heart create for me, O God, and a steadfast spirit renew within me" (Psalm 51:12).

4. Jesus' role in human reconciliation. We learn from the Bible that somehow the Lord Jesus is involved in the process of our aversion from sin and conversion to God. In Biblical language it is worded: "By his wounds you were healed" (1 Peter 2:24—see also Chap. 7: Reconciliation). The early Church brought this out clearly in the Scripture below: Matthew 9:1-8. Apparently, God wants to approach sinners also visibly. Just as Jesus was present to this sinner in this Gospel passage, so the Church, Sacrament of Jesus Christ, wishes to be present in the process of our conversion and reconciliation with God.

5. Reconciliation in the past. This presence of the Church in the process of reconciliation has not been equally tangible over the ages. During the first four centuries, the Church was visibly present only in some serious cases, that hurt also the institution, e.g., apostasy or openly living in adultery. In those cases, penance was a public affair. Penitent sinners were obliged to wear a hair shirt, ashes were sprinkled over their heads, and the bishop reconciled them with God and the Church on Holy Thursday.

This custom disappeared in the fifth century, to be replaced a few centuries later by a new way of being present to the sinner, namely, oral confession. It originated from counseling situations in the Irish and British monasteries. Counseling became sharing of guilt, hence oral confession, first as an option and later as a Church law. From Ireland and England oral confession spread over the continent of Europe. First, the new custom was fiercely opposed especially in Spain. Later, in was accepted and has endured to the present time: Confession of sin—short advice—absolution of sin—and penance to be done!

6. Reconciliation as a community affair. The Second Vatican Council made a few changes concerning oral confession. It wants to make reconciliation a community affair again by encouraging penitential services; and it wishes to restore the counseling element in confession by suggesting the option of "confession with prayerful dialogue," called "face to face confession," which requires some more time and is best done by appointment. In this way, penitent and confessor (counselor) can discuss quietly not just how to avoid sin but rather how to grow as a Christian. (See also p. 102.)

7. Bible reading

Jesus cures a paralytic

[Jesus] came back to his own town. There the people at once brought to him a paralyzed man lying on a mat. When Jesus saw their faith he said to the paralytic, "Have courage, son, your sins are forgiven." At that some of the scribes said to themselves, "The man blasphemes." Jesus was aware of what they were thinking and said: "Why do you harbor evil thoughts? Which is less trouble to say, 'Your sins are forgiven' or 'Stand up and walk'? To help you realize that the Son of Man has authority on earth to forgive sins"—he then said to the paralyzed man—"Stand up! Roll up your mat, and go home." The man stood up and went toward his home. At the sight, a feeling of awe came over the crowd, and they praised God for giving such authority to men.   *(Matthew 9:1-8)*

Jesus confers the power to forgive sins

On the evening of that first day of the week, even though the disciples had locked the doors of the place where they were for fear of the Jews, Jesus came and stood before them. "Peace be with you," he said. When he had said this, he showed them his hands and his side. At the sight of the Lord the disciples rejoiced. "Peace be with you," he said again.

"As the Father has sent me,
so I send you."
Then he breathed on them and said:
"Receive the Holy Spirit.
If you forgive men's sins,
they are forgiven them;
if you hold them bound,
they are held bound."   *(John 20:19-23)*

Questions for Discussion

1. How can evil cloud our vision?

2. Why is apologizing on the human level important for reconciliation with God?

3. Discuss how the Church was present to a Christian's reconciliation with God over the centuries.

17.
GOD'S HEALING PRESENCE

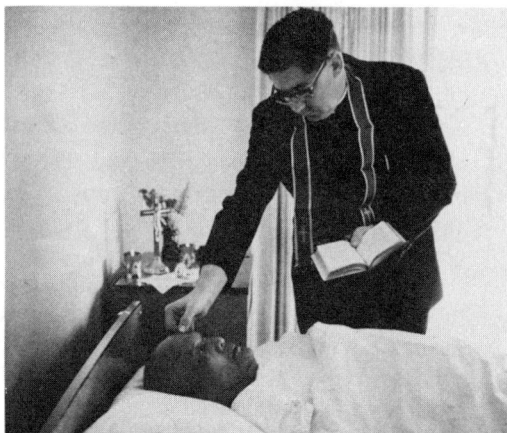

1. Clerical presence in hospitals. A hospital is the place where all the misery of town comes to a head. Hosts of helping hands, doctors, nurses, aides, relatives, and volunteers, try to alleviate pain. Healing is a profession. What is a chaplain doing in this setting? Besides reserved parking place for doctors, most hospitals also have a few spots reserved for the clergy. Seemingly, they want a clergyman to be there.

2. Presence of the Church. The Church deems it meaningful to be present as a sacrament, a sign of Jesus Christ, in all the important moments of life: birth, maturation, entering the marital state or ministry, moments of need for intimacy with the Divine, of need for reconciliation and healing. Psychosomatic beings as we are, we need more than surgery and "shots." We need the loving presence of fellow human beings.

Loneliness, helplessness, sin, guilt, and whatever may cause anguish and need healing as well. Christian doctors and nurses should be aware of their vocation to be present to their patients. All of us are the Church, all of us should be a sacrament of the healing Lord to old, lonely, sick people around us.

3. Symbolic anointing. During time of sickness, it is the Church's vocation to be present to an ailing fellow Christian. As the Lord Jesus prayed and underlined His prayer for the sick with symbolical actions (even using mud and saliva), the Church underlines her prayer for sick people with an anointing.

Television commercials and the shelves of your local drugstore proclaim that ointments are useful for soothing pain and healing. Thus, over the centuries, this healing presence of the Church became known as "Anointing of the Sick." Preferably, this assistance to the sick is given in a community setting: in a healing service in church or in the family. All of us are Church, all of us pray and receive, all of us celebrate together the healing presence of the Lord Jesus to His people.

4. Summary of the rite. In the ritual, we hear the Word which instructs, penetrates, and inspires. There is a reference to James 5:13-16. A penitential service, resulting in contrition, conditions the sick person to be healed, made whole, in both mind and body. Actually, I am my body, and as such in need of healing. We listen to one of the healing narratives, in which we experience the Lord Jesus as healer of humankind.

The laying on of hands stands for conveying the sacred, i.e., the healing power of God. We ask God to ease the patient's suffering and to strengthen him/her in pain and weakness. And the priest prays that, through the anointing, the Lord in His love and mercy may help our sick sister/brother with the grace of the Holy Spirit. In faith, we ask for the restoration of health—always leaving it up to God as to how He will heal—and finish the celebration by sharing the Eucharist.

5. Bible reading

Cure of the Centurion's Servant

As Jesus entered Capernaum, a centurion approached him with this request: "Sir, my serving boy is at home in bed paralyzed, suffering painfully." He said to him, "I will come and cure him." "Sir," the centurion said in reply, "I am not worthy to have you under my roof. Just give an order and my boy will get better. I am a man under authority myself and I have troops assigned to me. If I give one man the order, 'Dismissed,' off he goes. If I say to another, 'Come here,' he comes. If I tell my slave, 'Do this,' he does it." Jesus showed amazement on hearing this and remarked to his followers, "I assure you, I have never found this much faith in Israel."

To the centurion Jesus said, "Go home. It shall be done because you trusted." That very moment the boy got better.

(Matthew 8:5-13)

Questions for Discussion

1. Why and how should all Christians, doctors, nurses, priests, and lay people be present to sick persons.

2. As sacrament of Christ, how is the Church present in all important moments of life?

3. Discuss the statement: "It is up to God as to how He will heal a sick person."

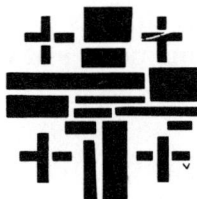

18. MINISTRY — SERVICE

1. Types of service. "It is our business to serve you"—and make a fortune in the process. Ads don't mention the second part of this statement. All want to *serve*, from the Internal Revenue Service to the local gas service station. The medical doctor *serves*, but before you get a chance to leave his office, his secretary presents you with a substantial bill.

It is the Queen's Prime Minister (servant) who rules England, and the Pope is called "The Servant of the servants of God." The leader of a Christian community too is often called minister, although names like pastor (shepherd), priest, and father are used as well. Is there a difference between the service which Christians offer to fellow human beings and the service which is "business"? There should be!

2. Service leaders in the early Church. What kind of service does God's people expect from its ministers? Expectations have not always been the same, and the New Testament leaves a great margin of freedom in this regard. In the ancient Church, a Christian community simply chose a leader from their midst. With neighboring leaders, bishops (overseers), and presbyters (elders), they laid hands on him and prayed to the Holy Spirit. Communion with the Church at large was understood as important. This leader presided also over the Eucharist.

There was never a shortage of priests, nor a congregation without regular celebration of the Eucharist. Whenever a leader resigned, he automatically returned to the state of lay person and was no longer entitled to preside over the Eucharistic celebration.

3. Origin of priests as leaders. Only later, in the fourth century, when the Eucharist was ever more seen as a sacrifice (see chap. 14: "The Eucharistic Celebration") and God's people grew in awareness of being a priestly people, were bishops first and later also presbyters (elders-leaders of local communities) seen as priests, related to cult, offering sacrifice.

These men were always leaders of a congregation. Ordination meant "insertion" into the order of an existing community of believers. Deacons were ordained more or less in the same way only without the presbyters being present, since they were exclusively in service of the local bishop.

4. Loss of idea of service. Although the Council of Chalcedon (451 A.D.) had forbidden to ordain men unless they were called by a congregation to be their leader, gradually, after 1000 A.D., the Roman Catholic Church began ordaining men without being called by a parish community. In that time private Masses became a custom. The dozens of altars in big churches still testify to this period. Priesthood was seen as a Divinely given power to consecrate the bread and the wine. The idea of ministry (service) faded away. Many ministers were just priests, i.e., "Mass sayers."

5. The man of the sanctuary. With slight variations, this was the priest-image elderly Catholics grew up with. The priest was seen as the man of the sanctuary, by both his celibate life style and his preoccupation with worship and Sacraments, segregated from the lay people, their man-in-between with God.

6. The model of Church ministry. The Second Vatican Council has opened the way for reconsidering this picture of our ministers. It suggests looking back to the early time of the Church, although it does not state that our ministers should be exactly as they were in the first three centuries of Christianity. Since our four Eucharistic Prayers and other prayers of the Roman Missal stress the sacrificial connotation of the Eucharist so much, we will go on seeing our ministers as priests. But their priestly occupation (presiding over the Eucharist) is only part of their ministry.

The model of all Church ministry is our Lord, Who came to serve and not to be served. "Power" was far from His mind. He served as healer, preacher, prophet, social reformer, counselor, and He was all of this with great dedication, even to the extent of giving up His life. Later theologians explained our Lord's life, suffering, and death as a sacrificial offering, which like a Jewish High Priest He offered to God for the remission of sins. Hence Jesus-Priest! The contemporary minister looks to this exemplar.

However, God's people must be reasonable. One man cannot possibly reflect all the facets of our Lord's ministry. Each minister has his own charisms and weaknesses. With love and understanding, we should accept him as he is with his limitations. And young people should accept the challenge, if they feel called tó serve God's people as ordained minister.

Since the willingness to serve as *celibate* ministers is dwindling rapidly, the request for a married and/or female clergy is heard quite often nowadays. As yet our leaders are hesitant to undo a longstanding tradition. Pray for God's guidance! Somehow a solution must be found.

Ponder where you fit in. In today's Church, there are many ministries: the ministry of priest or deacon, the ministry of word, altar, social concern, catechetics, youth, evangelization, etc. Perhaps your diocese offers training courses. Ask for information.

7. Bible reading

Tasks of an apostolic ministry

In the presence of God and of Christ Jesus, who is coming to judge the living and the dead, and by his appearing and his kingly power, I charge you to preach the word, to stay with this task whether convenient or inconvenient—correcting, reproving, appealing—constantly teaching and never losing patience. For the time will come when people will not tolerate sound doctrine, but, following their own desires, will surround themselves with teachers who tickle their ears. They will stop listening to the truth and will wander off to fables. As for you, be steady and self-possessed; put up with hardship, perform your work as an evangelist, fulfill your ministry.   *(2 Timothy 4:1-5)*

Questions for Discussion

1. What kind of service did God's people expect from its ministers in the past?
2. Discuss the relationship between ministry, leadership, and priesthood.
3. What is your image of a contemporary minister?

19. MARRIAGE IN CHRIST

1. Celebration in common There are moments in life when we don't want to be alone. This may be a time of extreme sorrow (death, funeral) or abundant joy. A wedding is such a moment. We want to celebrate with relatives and friends, who were invited to be the happy witnesses and sharers of our gladness and bliss.

2. Presence of the Church. The Church, being the sacrament of Christ, deems it very useful and important to be in the wedding party when a young couple is going to make the commitment to "go it together" for life. As the Lord Jesus was present at the wedding in Cana with His loving care, so the Church, being an extension of Christ, wants to be present at the weddings of her members.

This presence of the Church at weddings has not always been as visible as it is nowadays. For centuries Christians married merely in accord with their local customs, although the Church has always reminded couples to reflect in their married lives the love of Christ for His Church (all of us) and the other way around.

71

(See Bible reading below!) Later it became a custom for young couples to go to the priest for a blessing. Much later, that blessing and the eventual addition of the exchange of marital vows in the presence of a priest became Church law.

As things stand now, Catholic couples make their mutual commitment with three witnesses present, one of them being an authorized priest. Only if a priest is not available for a long time, two witnesses suffice to be married legally in the eyes of the Church.

3. Presence of God in marriage. This required presence of the Church should be seen as a concern to signify Christ's presence at the very important moment of a wedding. It is a presence married people should always foster and be aware of all of their lives together. The mutual intimacy of husband and wife should not be seen as intruded upon by Christ's—God's—presence.

God, the Maker of love, sex, and the whole human person, wants married people to be happy and celebrate their mutual love sexually. Married people should meet God in one another's eyes! Rather than seeing sex as something that distracts from intimacy with God, they should enjoy it as a beautiful gift of the Maker.

4. Love and communication. Love, kept alive by constant communication, should be the guiding principle in married life. Sex is just one of the means of communication and it should always be an expression of love. Animals mate, but human beings make love. It is quite a difference!

For details on all of this: love, alienation, sexual problems, responsible parenthood, and means of birth control, turn to your instructor, priest, psychologist, or marriage counselor. Whenever signs of alienation set in, ask for help! Many people die of cancer because they waited too long before they consulted a doctor.

5. Rite of marriage. The marriage ritual recalls the dignity and beauty of married life by quoting the Bible and it states that Christ abundantly blesses marital love. The couple promises one another fidelity for better, for worse, for richer, for poorer, in sickness and in health, until death parts them.

The congregation prays with the couple for the sanctity of Christian marriage, school of perfection, and for all homemakers. There is a special nuptial blessing, asking God to look with love upon this woman and her husband. And ideally (not easily to be skipped!) sharing the Liturgy with the Lord and all present should be part of the celebration.

6. Bible reading

Duties of Christian spouses

Be imitators of God as his dear children. Follow the way of love, even as Christ loved you. He gave himself for us as an offering to God, a gift of pleasing fragrance.

Husbands, love your wives, as Christ loved the church. He gave himself up for her to make her holy, purifying her in the bath of water by the power of the word, to present to himself a glorious church, holy and immaculate, without stain or wrinkle or anything of that sort. Husbands should love their wives as they do their own bodies. He who loves his wife loves himself. Observe that no one ever hates his own flesh; no, he nourishes it and takes care of it as Christ cares for the church—for we are members of his body.

> "For this reason a man shall leave his father and mother,
>   and shall cling to his wife,
>   and the two shall be made into one."

This is a great foreshadowing; I mean that it refers to Christ and the Church.   *(Ephesians 5:1-2, 25-32)*

Excellence of the gift of love

Now I will show you the way which surpasses all the others. If I speak with human tongues and angelic as well, but do not have love, I am a noisy gong, a clanging cymbal. If I have the gift of prophecy and, with full knowledge, comprehend all mysteries, if I have faith great enough to move mountains, but have not love, I am nothing. If I give everything I have to feed the poor and hand over my body to be burned, but have not love, I gain nothing.

Love is patient; love is kind. Love is not jealous, it does not put on airs, it is not snobbish. Love is never rude, it is not self-seeking, it is not prone to anger; neither does it brood over injuries. Love does not rejoice in what is wrong but rejoices with the truth. There is no limit to love's forbearance, to its trust, its hope, its power to endure.   *(1 Corinthians 13:1-7)*

Questions for Discussion

1. Why does the Church want to be present at a wedding?

2. Discuss why marital intimacy should not be in conflict with intimacy with God.

3. What should couples do when the first signs of alienation set in?

20. SACRAMENTAL LANGUAGE

1. Symbolic actions. Pro-lifers are handing out red roses. At a mass rally the effigy of a hated politician is burned. In Vietnam a Buddhist monk sets himself on fire. At Christmas we exchange gifts. When we meet, we shake hands, hug, or kiss one another. We send flowers to a friend in the hospital.

All of these are symbolic actions intended to make a point in the most vivid way possible. Why don't we use just plain language? Why do we make use of symbols? Why do we underline a statement with a symbolic action?

2. Concrete language. The reason seems to be the old adage that "actions speak louder than words," and the fact that certain things cannot be communicated simply by words. Connected with this is the observation that earthly things have the capacity to signify something other than themselves or something other than what they show at first glance.

In time of severe drought, the farmer experiences rain-water as life-giving, for it saves his crop. Oil placed on a sore wound is experienced as soothing and causing a good feeling all over. Fire warms and also contributes to a homey mood when burning in an open fireplace at Christmas. These "earthly things" can be used to signify the experiences with which they are associated and which are beyond perception, e.g., water as life-giving, oil as healing, and fire as suggesting God's presence in light, love, and intimacy.

We should keep heart and mind open for the language of symbols. Do you enjoy good music or a beautiful poem? Keep alive the intuition of the artist in you because only then can you savor the religious symbolism which is the language of the sacraments.

3. Divine symbols. Observing these facts, we should try to understand the way Almighty God tries to communicate with human beings. The symbols He uses are adapted to human intelligence. He utilizes the experience of a people, as we possess it in its sacred literature, the Bible, and above all the most outstanding specimen that came forth from this people: Jesus of Nazareth. We see Him as the Sacrament (sign, symbol) of the encounter with God.

4. Church symbols. Likewise the Church, being the extension of our Lord in this world, is seen as a sign or Sacrament of God's loving presence. We experience this loving presence of God in symbols adapted to our intelligence. Some of these symbols received a special significance in the Christian tradition: a meal, washing, anointing, laying on of hands, marriage vows, all of them very fundamental elements in people's lives. Christ and the Church designated these elements as effective symbols of a sacred reality, namely, God present, giving Himself, and communicating with human beings.

5. Sacraments and grace. Viewing the Sacraments as means of communication of God with human beings, we should keep in mind that these symbols are not magic tricks to produce "something" in us which could be called "grace." Communication is not a magic trick. It is a two-way, give-and-take, affair between two persons. God approaches you in a symbol and you respond in Faith. Moreover, grace is not "something." Grace is that interpersonal relationship with God, analogous to the relationship between friends.

6. Sacraments—different aspects of God's presence. When I visit a friend in the hospital, I am present to him in a way different from when I attended his wedding. By using different Sacraments, the Church shows us different aspects of God's presence. In other words, the Church wants you to experience God adapted to your particular needs.

When in need for intimacy, we Christians celebrate table fellowship with the Lord in the symbolism of bread and wine. When in need of healing, we celebrate the anointing of the sick and experience God as healer. Concentrate on this perspective whenever Sacraments or sacramentals (like holy water, incense, blessings) are used to symbolize God's presence. (See also p. 98.)

7. Bible reading

Jesus raises a little girl to life

Before Jesus had finished speaking to them, a synagogue leader came up, did him reverence, and said: "My daughter has just died. Please come and lay your hand on her and she will come back to life." Jesus stood up and followed him, and his disciples did the same.

When Jesus arrived at the synagogue leader's house and saw the flute prayers and the crowd who were making a din, he said, "Leave, all of you! The little girl is not dead. She is asleep." At this they began to ridicule him. When the crowd has been put out he entered and took her by the hand and the little girl got up. News of this circulated throughout the district.

(Matthew 9:18-19, 23-26)

Questions for Discussion

1. Why do we use symbols? Discuss examples!

2. Discuss some Sacraments and how their symbolism points to the transcendent.

3. Discuss the various ways God/Christ/the Church is present to you in Sacraments and sacramentals.

"I will meditate on your precepts and consider your ways" (Ps 119:15).
The Thinker. Sculpture by Rodin (1840-1917), France.

21. LOVE AS ROOT AND FOUNDATION

1. Need for energy and motivation. Cars need fuel to keep going. Plants need fertilizer to grow. We humans eat to remain physically healthy. And we need motivation to function as total human beings. Lacking the stamina to take initiatives is a sign of aging. It could be the reason why society puts most people of sixty-five gently on a side track.

2. Love as primary motivation. What motivates you? The reward-and-punishment syndrome plays an important role at the beginning of life, and, sad to say, in many an adult life as well. The determination to make a living and support a family is good of course, but greed is un-Christian and fear of punishment puerile. The challenge to make love the main motivation of your do's and dont's is what you accepted when you joined the Christian movement. Only when you take this challenge seriously, are you a Christian worth your salt.

3. Function of laws and commandments. The challenge of love sounds good. But what about laws and commandments? When in each situation of my life I ask: "What is the loving thing to do?" why do I need laws? Laws and commandments are clarifications of what exactly "the loving thing to do" is in each situation. And as such they are needed.

If all of us were so mature in Christ that the compass of love would point out the direction unfalteringly, we could do without laws that explain the ramifications of love in the various human situations. But such maturity of love is rather rare. We need the laws that reflect the wisdom of fellow humans over the years. They are helpful beacons in our dark and often confused situations.

However, when adult Christians have to make a decision of conscience, they will not evade their responsibility by depending blindly on the letter of the law. Rather they will listen to what the law can provide as a correction of their own views. For more on laws, see the following chapters!

4. Love of self, God, and neighbor. A vice that plagues all organized religion is legalism. Do nothing more than you must do (just the minimum!), avoid mortal sin and save your soul! As if Christianity were just a system for saving one's soul! This is a far cry from the beautiful child-father relationship which Jesus wants our relationship with God to be.

Love should be the root and foundation of your life! (See Ephesians 3:14-21, below.) First love of yourself: You cannot love anybody, if you don't love yourself as a precious child of the heavenly Father, worth being loved. And then love of God and neighbor! "What you do to the least of my brothers you do for me!" Read Matthew 25:31-46 prayerfully!

5. Bible reading

Christ's surpassing love

That is why I kneel before the Father from whom every family in heaven and on earth takes its name; and I pray that he will bestow on you gifts in keeping with the riches of his glory. May he strengthen you inwardly through the working of his Spirit. May Christ dwell in your hearts through faith, and may charity be the root and foundation of your life. Thus you will be able to grasp fully, with all the holy ones, the breadth and length and height and depth of Christ's love, and experience this love which surpasses all knowledge, so that you may attain to the fullness of God himself.

To him whose power now at work in us can do immeasurably more than we ask or imagine—to him be glory in the church and in Christ Jesus through all generations, world without end. Amen.   *(Ephesians 3:14-21)*

Questions for Discussion

1. Besides the syndrome mentioned in number 2, above, what other motivations to act do you know? For example, discuss: revenge, "proving yourself," jealousy, pride.

2. What about "doing the right thing for the wrong reason"? Discuss examples and relate them to "love as root and foundation."

3. Why do we need laws? Discuss examples.

22. GOOD AND BAD CONSCIENCE

1. Capacity for right moral judgment. During the war in Vietnam, we read about "conscientious" objectors, citizens who in good conscience refused to be drafted and go to fight that war on the other side of the Pacific. We speak of a good and a bad "conscience," an erroneous "conscience," a well-educated or poorly-educated "conscience."

What is conscience? Theologians and psychologists quarrel about details, but we may state that every new-born child has a capacity for right moral judgment, just as it has a capacity for speech and interpreting sight and sound. How this capacity will be developed depends on the child's education. Hence, whenever we deal with the conscience of an adolescent or adult, we deal with an already more or less educated conscience. Education from early childhood on and self-education as a life-time job are of decisive importance.

2. An erroneous conscience. When a child is brought up and trained in theft, sexual license, and murder, we may assume that he considers his behavior as right. His is an *erroneous* conscience. More or less the same can be stated about people living outside the impact of the Christian outlook on behavior. Their "capacity for moral judgment" is also shaped through the environment they are born into. As long as they honestly follow their conscience, they are good people and we should not judge them when their behavior is different from what we consider as right.

3 A Christian conscience. A Christian's conscience is formed by a Christian environment: family, parish, school, society. The Christian environment is marked by the presence of Christ. The mysterious presence of our Lord—in fellow Christians, the Bible, the signs (Sacraments) He left us—and the guidance of the Church form a Christian conscience. In this environment love for God in Christ develops your capacity for right moral judgment (conscience).

It is clear, then, that Christians who follow their conscience must know Christ and what He stands for. The more Christians are mature and well informed, the more they will be guided by real love and the less they will need the many laws that clarify the implications and ramifications of love of God and neighbor.

4. Approach based on law. There are various ways of approaching the question of how to behave as a Christian. Firstly, we have the way of traditional catechisms. Usually, our traditional catechisms take the law as a starting point. You learn the Commandments and simply follow them. When you have a problem, you ask your confessor and do whatever he tells you is right. This is often the easiest way. It does not require a growth into maturity, and you do not have to inform yourself. "Father told me..." is what you go by.

5. Approach based on conscience guided by love. Another way is to take as a starting point your unique situation and conscience, guided by love. But then you accept the duty of keeping yourself informed.

Growing to Christian adulthood is a lifetime job. Forming your conscience is a lifelong search to discover what God is asking of you in your concrete situation.

This way of "freedom" is not the easier way, since it sets you free only for a deeper commitment. Ever more Christians in the Catholic tradition accept this challenge. They study the charming personality of our Lord, as the early Church presents Him in the New Testament and commit themselves to go by what He stands for.

Accepting this challenge does not mean that all must have a Ph.D. in theology. An average education and the will to search is enough. Neither does this approach make the Commandments and counseling superfluous, as we have mentioned already in Chapter 21. Rather it is a question of emphasis: first comes love and then the rules entailed in it—not the other way around.

6. Bible reading

Moral goodness

How shall a young man be faultless in his way?
  By keeping to your words.
With all my heart I seek you;
  let me not stray from your commands.
Within my heart I treasure your promise,
  that I may not sin against you.
Blessed are you, O Lord;
  teach me your statutes.   *(Psalm 119:9-12)*

Questions for Discussion

1. Discuss cases of conscientious objection (draft, abortion, euthanasia, contraception.)

2. How do you form your conscience?

3. Discuss the two ways of approaching the question of how to behave as a Christian. What is your preference and why?

23. LOVE AND LAW

1. Need for laws. We are proud that our country is based on laws, a sound and wise constitution, and law enforcement. We may not agree with all the bills our lawmakers turn out when in session, but we agree that we need laws. Law enforcement officers may not be courteous all the time, but we can't do without them. And we need lawyers and judges.

The Church as institution has canon law tribunals and canon lawyers. And the first five books of the Bible are called "The Law of Moses." Jesus has said: "I did not come to do away with the Law," but He has stated also that the whole law is based on the great commandment of love for God and neighbor (Matthew 22:37-40).

2. Relationship of love and Commandments. This last statement of Jesus may be a good starting point to discuss the relationship between love and the Commandments. To begin with, no law has meaning if it cannot be seen as a ramification (interpretation) of the great law of love. It is sad to say, but it can happen that legislators make laws which are incompatible with the law of love. (For example, there is a law in Southern states that a black person cannot marry a white one!)

85

In such a case, you are not bound by the law. Your informed conscience must guide you. (See chap. 22.) But the fact that there may be some unjust laws does not mean that you should not be a law-abiding citizen. In our society, law is just an alternative to chaos. If we need laws, we should obey them.

3. Laws of the Old Testament. As for laws in the Bible, the Old Testament relates many laws. Actually, the first five books are called "The Law." Figuratively, the Bible relates these laws to Moses and Mount Sinai. In reality, these laws originated gradually in the Hebrew communities. They reflect what the collective Hebrew mind, guided by God, considered as good and evil. When reading laws in the Bible, you should remember that many of them are conditioned by time and culture. These laws do not bind us. (See, for example, Exodus 21:1-37; 22:1-30.) Other laws are related to the human condition as such. These are to be paid attention to. (See Deuteronomy 5:6-21; 6:4-6; Exodus 20:2-17.) (See also p. 100.)

4. Laws of the New Testament. As far as the New Testament is concerned, the early Christians meditated on Jesus of Nazareth, His personality, His sayings, and most of all His behavior in the daily events of life. These reflections on the Christ event were inspired (guided) by God. You should know the New Testament with its approach to behavioral problems. For example, read Matthew 5.

Since the ethical experience of God's people as related in the Bible was inspired (guided) by God, it is normative also for us. Human situations usually have something in common. This "something in common," found in any passage of Scripture, is called existential understanding. This understanding, related to *your* existence or life-situation, is decisive for faithful Bible reading.

5. Laws of the Church. What about Church law, e.g., partaking in the Eucharistic celebration every week, marrying before three witnesses, one of them an authorized priest, and a few more? We accept them by the fact that we are members of the Church. Moreover, we observe that the Biblical experience of 2000 years ago does not relate to all the problems of the 20th Century life. (See also pp. 100-101.)

Think of the birth control issue, a new understanding of marriage and sexuality (tied solely to procreation and/or as a value in its own right—a means of self-realization?), a new outlook on authority, implications of personhood (e.g., the woman a century ago and the working woman now!), euthanasia (mercy killing), sterilization, artificial insemination, abortion (at what stage can the fetus be regarded as a human person with full human rights?), capital punishment, nuclear war, the use of drugs, the ethics of modern business, the race issue, and responsibility for developing countries.

Concerning these ethical issues, God's people expects guidelines from the teaching authority of the Church, as embodied in the bishops with their head, the Bishop of Rome. An adult Christian should be acquainted with these rules and guidelines as expressed in papal encyclicals and documents of regional bishops' conferences.

6. Following one's conscience. All these above guidelines should be taken into consideration when you form your conscience. And remember well, after you have done all of this, *you* must make up *your* mind and decide what the loving thing is that should be done in *your* situation. The Church teaches that even an erroneous conscience must be followed. Only take care that yours is not erroneous because of your own fault!

7. Bible reading

The great commandment

"Hear, O Israel! The Lord is our God, the Lord alone! Therefore, you shall love the Lord, your God, with all your heart, and with all your soul, and with all your strength! Take to heart these words which I enjoin on you today. Drill them into your children. Speak of them at home and abroad, whether you are busy or at rest. Bind them at your wrist as a sign and let them be as a pendant on your forehead. Write them on the doorposts of your houses and on your gates."   *(Deuteronomy 6:4-9)*

Instruction to Children

"Later on, when your sons aks you what these ordinances, statutes and decrees mean which the Lord, our God, has enjoined on you, you shall say to your son, 'We were once slaves of Pharaoh in Egypt, but the Lord brought us out of Egypt with his strong hand and wrought before our eyes signs and wonders, great and dire, against Egypt and against Pharaoh and his whole house. He brought us from there to lead us into the land he promised on oath to our fathers, and to give it to us. Therefore, the Lord commanded us to observe all these statutes in fear of the Lord, our God, that we may always have as prosperous and happy a life as we have today; and our justice before the Lord, our God, is to consist in carefully observing all these commandments he has enjoined on us.' "   *(Deuteronomy 6:20-25)*

Questions for Discussion

1. Discuss some civil laws and how they can/cannot be related to the law of love.

2. Find some laws in the Bible which certainly do not bind us anymore. Discuss why not!

3. Discuss some of the guidelines of the Church on issues mentioned under no. 5.

"Lord, for your faithful people life is changed, not ended."

24. THE JOURNEY FROM WHICH THERE IS NO RETURN

1. Death awaits all. In the morality play of the same name, *Everyman* (all of us) is reminded by *Death* that he will soon have to make the journey from which there is no return. He protests that death is farthest from his thoughts at the time. *Death* is adamant but assures *Everyman* that he can take any companions who want to make the journey with him.

Weeping at his plight, *Everyman* thinks of *Fellowship* with whom he has spent so many pleasant days in sport and play. *Fellowship* answers that he would be willing to go with *Everyman* for sport or play or to seek lusty women, but he refuses to go on that long journey. Then *Everyman* asks *Kindred* (his relatives) who replies that he would go willingly if it were not for a cramp in his toe. Finally *Everyman* asks *Good-Deeds* to go with him, but *Good-Deeds* is lying on the cold ground, bound by sins. It is *Knowledge* who guides *Everyman* to confession. After *Everyman* does penance, *Good-Deeds* rises up from the ground and is the only companion who accompanies *Everyman* on his journey to face *Death*.

2. Death in Scripture. Thinking of death, judgment, and life hereafter, we want to know details. Formerly, the solution was suggested that "the soul" was separated from "the body." The soul goes on existing, while the body decays. The Bible does not speak of such a clear-cut distinction of soul and body. "Soul" means most of all "you," of which Jesus said: "This day *you* will be with me" (Luke 23:43). Actually, the only thing we can say is: "Existence after death is already somehow like the resurrection of our new body. It is the coming to light of what existed already during our lifetime on earth, namely, our communion with God, which even death cannot destroy. Our oneness with God bears within it the germ of the resurrection. Life is changed not taken away." That is all. Scripture does not instruct us as to exactly "how" future life will be.

3. Hell. Jesus Christ has revealed that "hell" is possible, since man can abuse his freedom. He has never said that there are persons who have been condemned or will be condemned for all eternity. Christ's message, inspired by love, warns us of the possibility that a free person can turn away from God deliberately. A condemned person judges himself, since he refuses God's offer of love. Death simply permanentizes that person's adhesion to evil and aversion from God. Scripture uses images of fire, darkness, and gnashing of teeth! Hell means "no God"—"no love."

4. Purgatory. To pray for the deceased is a tradition in the Church. Why do we pray for our dearly beloved who passed away? We do so because there is so much ill-will and inclination to evil in a person, even if he dies in grace. There is so much to be purged from man's inborn egotism. This happens through death. How long does this "purge" last? Again we must say that this happens outside our concept of time.

After death there is no "time" any longer. Formerly, "purgatory" was visualized as a fire. We should go back to the old Christian concept and see this "purge" as belonging to death, as perhaps happening in death itself. This would not make prayer for the dead senseless, since our prayer overlaps time, just as Christ's redemption affects us as well as people of thousands of years ago.

5. Heaven. Reward is mentioned in Scripture, but not in such a way as if heaven is a paycheck for a good life. Heaven is what you have made of yourself, with the help of God, of course, in this life! As such "heaven" is a reward.

6. Eternal life. We believe in the resurrection of the body, which does not mean "from mortal remains." "You," as described under number 2, will go on existing. The Bible uses visionary language to describe our collective existence for all eternity with God. Again, do not think too much about how, when, and where these things will happen. Since these things happen outside our concept of time we cannot speak of "time" in between judgment at our death and "last judgment." We do not know "how" this is or will be.

More important is St. Paul's advice to us, as long as we live in this world: "[We must] reject godless ways and worldly desires, and live temperately, justly, and devoutly in this age as we await our blessed hope, the appearing of the glory of the great God and of our Savior Christ Jesus" (Titus 2:12-13).

7. Bible reading

Divine Beatitude

"Never again shall they know hunger or thirst,
nor shall the sun or its heat beat down on them,
for the Lamb on the throne will shepherd them.
He will lead them to springs of life-giving water,
and God will wipe every tear from their eyes."

(Revelation 7:16-17)

God—all in all

Just as in Adam all die, so in Christ all come to life again, but
each one in proper order: Christ the first fruits and then, at his
coming, all those who belong to him. After that will come the
end, when, after having destroyed every sovereignty, authority, and power, he will hand over the kingdom to God the
Father.

When, finally, all has been subjected to the Son, he will then
subject himself to the One who made all things subject to him,
so that God may be all in all.   *(1 Corinthians 15:22-24, 28)*

New Heavens and New Earth

Then I saw new heavens and a new earth. The former
heavens and the former earth had passed away, and the sea
was no longer. I also saw a new Jerusalem, the holy city, coming down out of heaven from God, beautiful as a bride prepared
to meet her husband. I heard a loud voice from the throne cry
out: "This is God's dwelling among men. He shall dwell with
them and they shall be his people and he shall be their God who
is always with them. He shall wipe every tear from their eyes,
and there shall be no more death or mourning, crying out or
pain, for the former world has passed away."

(Revelation 21:1-4)

Questions for Discussion

1. Discuss Revelation 14:13 and the statement that "heaven"
   is not just a paycheck for a good life.

2. Discuss Matthew 22:2-10, in which Jesus compares
   heaven to a wedding-feast, in the perspective of what is
   said under no. 5

3. Discuss Paul's description of the endtime in 1 Corinthians
   15:22-24, 28 and relate it to the statement under no. 5.

Appendices

It is important that parents and teachers be aware of the following directive:

In every age and culture Christianity has commended certain prayers, formulas, and practices to all members of the faith community, even the youngest. While catechesis cannot be limited to the repetition of formulas and it is essential that formulas and facts pertaining to faith be understood, memorization has nevertheless had a special place in the handing-on of the faith throughout the ages and should continue to have such a place today, especially in catechetical programs for the young. It should be adapted to the level and ability of the child and introduced in a gradual manner, through a process which, begun early, continues gradually, flexibly, and never slavishly. In this way certain elements of Catholic faith, tradition, and practice are learned for a lifetime and can contribute to the individual's continued growth in understanding and living the faith.

Among these are the following:

1.   Prayers such as the Sign of the Cross, Lord's Prayer, Hail Mary, Apostles' Creed, Acts of Faith, Hope and Charity, Act of Contrition.

2.   Factual information contributing to an appreciation of the place of the word of God in the Church and the life of the Christian through an awareness and understanding of: the key themes of the history of salvation; the major personalities of the Old and New Testaments; and certain biblical texts expressive of God's love and care.

3.   Formulas providing factual information regarding worship, the Church Year, and major feasts of our Lord and our Lady, the various eucharistic devotions, the mysteries of the rosary of the Blessed Virgin Mary, and the Stations of the Cross.

4.   Formulas and practices dealing with the moral life of Christians including the commandments, the beatitudes, the gifts of the Holy Spirit, the theological and moral virtues, the precepts of the Church, and the examination of conscience.   (National Catechetical Directory,176e)

APPENDIX 1
ESSENTIAL PRAYERS

Sign of the Cross

IN the name of the Father, and the Son, and of the Holy Spirit. Amen.

The Lord's Prayer

OUR Father, who art in heaven, hallowed be thy name; thy kingdom come; thy will be done on earth as it is in heaven. Give us this day our daily bread; and forgive us our trespasses as we forgive those who trespass against us; and lead us not into temptation, but deliver us from evil. Amen.

Hail Mary

HAIL Mary, full of grace! The Lord is with you; blessed are you among women, and blessed is the fruit of your womb, Jesus. Holy Mary, Mother of God, pray for us sinners, now and at the hour of our death. Amen.

Doxology

GLORY be to the Father, and to the Son and to the Holy Spirit. As it was in the beginning, is now, and ever shall be, world without end. Amen.

The Apostles' Creed

I BELIEVE in God the Father Almighty, Creator of heaven and earth; And in Jesus Christ, his only Son, our Lord; who was conceived by the Holy Spirit, born of the Virgin Mary; suffered under Pontius Pilate, was crucified, died, and was buried; he descended into hell; the third day he rose again from the dead; he ascended into heaven, and sits at the right hand of God the Father Almighty; from thence he shall come to judge the living and the dead. I believe in the Holy Spirit; the Holy Catholic Church; the Communion of Saints; the forgiveness of sins; the resurrection of the body; and life everlasting. Amen.

Act of Faith

O MY God, I firmly believe all the truths that the holy Catholic Church believes and teaches; I believe these truths, O Lord, because you, the infallible Truth, have revealed them to her; in this faith I am resolved to live and die. Amen.

Act of Hope

O MY God, trusting in your promises, and because you are faithful, powerful and merciful, I hope, through the merits of Christ, for the pardon of my sins, final perseverance, and the blessed glory of heaven. Amen.

Act of Charity

O MY God, because you are infinite Goodness and worthy of infinite love, I love you with my whole heart above all things, and for love of you, I love my fellowmen as myself. Amen.

Act of Contrition

O MY God, I am heartily sorry for having offended you, and I detest all my sins, because of your just punishments, but most of all because they offend you, my God, who are all good and deserving of all my love. I firmly resolve, with the help of your grace, to sin no more and to avoid the near occasions of sin.

Hail, Holy Queen

HAIL, holy Queen, Mother of mercy; hail our life, our sweetness, and our hope. To you do we cry, poor banished children of Eve. To you do we send up our sighs, mourning and weeping in this valley of tears. Turn then, most gracious Advocate, your eyes of mercy toward us. And after this our exile show unto us the blessed fruit of your womb, Jesus. O clement, O loving, O sweet Virgin Mary.

The Angelus

THE Angel of the Lord declared to Mary
And she conceived by the Holy Spirit. Hail Mary . . .

Behold the handmaid of the Lord.
Be it done to me according to your word. Hail Mary . . .
And the Word was made flesh.
And dwelt among us. Hail Mary . . .
Pray for us, O holy Mother of God.
That we may be made worthy of the promises of Christ.

Let us pray

POUR forth, we beseech you, O Lord, your grace into our hearts; that as we have known the incarnation of Christ, your Son, by the message of the angel, so by his Passion and Cross, we may be brought to the glory of his resurrection. Through the same Christ our Lord. Amen.

Grace before Meals

BLESS us, O Lord, and these your gifts which we are about to receive from your bounty. Through Christ our Lord. Amen.

Grace after Meals

WE give you thanks, Almighty God, for all your benefits, who live and reign world without end. Amen.

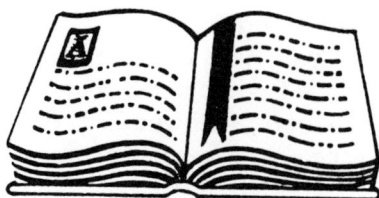

APPENDIX 2
THE HOLY BIBLE
"THE BIBLE IS THE WORD OF GOD ... IN THE LANGUAGE OF MAN"

● *What is the Bible?*

The Bible is a collection of sacred books, which were composed under the positive influence of the Holy Spirit by men chosen by God, and which have been accepted by the Church as inspired.

● *Who is the principal author of the Bible?*

God is the principal author of the Bible.

● *When and where was the Bible written?*

The Bible was written at various times and at various places by men chosen for this purpose by God.

● *How many books are in the Bible?*

In the Bible, as we know it, there are seventy-three books; forty-six books are in the Old Testament and twenty-seven in the New Testament.

● *If the Bible is written by men, why do we say that it is the Word of God?*

We say that the Bible is the Word of God because God inspired the men who wrote it.

● *Why is the Bible more excellent than any other book?*

The Bible is more excellent than any other book because God is its author and it centers around the mystery of the redemption of man.

● *How is the Old Testament related to the mystery of the redemption?*

The Old Testament describes the remote preparation for the coming of the Messiah.

● *Who are some of the outstanding people in the Old Testament?*

Abraham, our father in the faith; Moses, leader of God's people; David, King and Psalmist; and Isaiah, the Prophet of the Messiah.

● *How is the New Testament related to the mystery of the redemption?*

The New Testament describes the nature of the Messiah and tells the story of His redemptive mission.

● *Who are some of the outstanding people of the New Testament?*

Jesus Christ, the Son of God; Mary, his Virgin Mother; Peter, the Head of Christ's Church; and Paul, the Apostle who brought the Church to all people.

● *Can we really know and love Christ unless we study the Bible?*

No, we cannot know and love Christ unless we study the Bible because as Saint Augustine has said: "The New Testament is hidden in the Old Testament, and the Old Testament throws light on the New." Saint Jerome said: "Not to know the Bible is not to know Christ."

APPENDIX 3

THE LITURGY

The Church Year

EACH year through the Liturgy (especially the Mass), the Church makes present for us the Life, Death, and Resurrection of Jesus. In this way, we can encounter our Lord in his Mysteries, give glory to God, and obtain graces for ourselves and the whole world.

Outline of the Church Year

Advent — *Jesus is near.*
Christmas — *Jesus is with us.*
Epiphany — *Jesus shows his glory.*
Ordinary Time — *Jesus gives lessons for his Church.*
Lent — *Jesus suffers and dies for us.*
Easter — *Jesus triumphs over sin and death.*
Easter Time — *Jesus instructs his apostles.*
Ascension — *Jesus ascends to his heavenly Father.*
Pentecost — *Jesus sends the Holy Spirit.*
Ordinary Time — *The Spirit carries on the work of Jesus through his Church.*

Holy Mass

ON the Cross Jesus offered his body and blood to God the Father for us. In the Mass this great act is renewed for our benefit. We offer Jesus to God the Father in adoration, thanksgiving, reparation, and petition. We receive Jesus back from the Father as our Bread for eternal life. We sing hymns to praise God and to show our joy at Mass.

Major Parts of Holy Mass

Introductory Rites — *We speak to God in acts of contrition, praise, and petition.*

Liturgy of the Word — *We listen to what God says to us in the Readings, the Gospel, and the Homily.*

Liturgy of the Eucharist —

    Preparation of the Gifts — *With the priest we present the gifts of bread and wine.*

    Eucharistic Prayer — *At the consecration this bread and wine are changed into the Body and Blood of Jesus.*

    Communion Rite — *We receive Jesus who has given himself in love.*

Concluding Rite — *We receive God's blessing and go forth to bring Jesus to others.*

The Seven Sacraments

Baptism	Anointing of the Sick
Confirmation	Holy Orders
Holy Eucharist	Matrimony
Penance	

Holy Days of Obligation
in the United States

All Sundays of the year
January 1—Solemnity of Mary, Mother of God
Ascension of our Lord (forty days after Easter)
August 15—Assumption of the Blessed Virgin Mary
November 1—All Saints' Day
December 8—The Immaculate Conception
December 25—Christmas Day.

Major Feasts of Jesus and Mary

The major events of the Redemption are recalled in the feasts of Christ and find echoes in the feasts of Mary.

Jesus	*Mary*
Annunciation (Mar. 25)	— Immaculate Conception (Dec. 8)
Birth (Dec. 25)	— Birth (Sept. 8)
Presentation (Feb. 2)	— Presentation (Nov. 21)
Passion and Death (holy Week)	— Seven Sorrows (Sept. 15)
Resurrection (Easter Sun.)	— Assumption (Aug. 15)
Kingship (Last Sun. of Year)	— Queenship (Aug. 22)
Sacred Heart (Friday after Corpus Christi)	— Immaculate Heart (Saturday after Sacred Heart)
Body of Christ (Corpus Christi) (Sunday after Pentecost)	— Motherhood of Mary (Jan. 1)

Devotions to the Blessed Sacrament

AFTER Mass, Jesus remains in the tabernacles of our churches so that the sick who could not be present at Mass may also receive him. He also is there to receive our adoration in the rite of Benediction of the Blessed Sacrament. Finally, he is there so that we can visit him and draw strength and consolation from his presence.

The Mysteries of the Rosary

The Joyful Mysteries
1. The Annunciation of the Archangel Gabriel to Mary.
2. The Visitation of the Virgin Mary.
3. The Birth of Our Lord at Bethlehem.
4. The Presentation of Our Lord in the Temple.
5. The Finding of Our Lord in the Temple.

The Sorrowful Mysteries
1. The Agony of Our Lord in Garden of Gethsemane.
2. The Scourging of Our Lord at the pillar.
3. The crowning of Our Lord with thorns.
4. The carrying of the Cross by Our Lord to Calvary.
5. The Crucifixion and Death of Our Lord.

The Glorious Mysteries
1. The Resurrection of Our Lord from the dead.
2. The Ascension of Our Lord into Heaven.
3. Descent of the Holy Spirit upon the Apostles.
4. The Assumption of Mary into Heaven.
5. Crowning of Mary as Queen of Heaven.

Stations of the Cross

1. Pilate condemns Jesus.
2. Jesus takes his cross.
3. Jesus falls to the ground for the first time.
4. Jesus meets his Mother.
5. Simon helps Jesus carry his cross.
6. Veronica wipes the face of Jesus.
7. Jesus falls for the second time.
8. Jesus meets the women of Jerusalem.
9. Jesus falls for the third time.
10. The soldiers tear off Jesus' clothes.
11. Jesus is nailed to the cross.
12. Jesus dies on the cross.
13. Jesus is taken from the cross.
14. Jesus is laid in the tomb.

APPENDIX 4

CHRISTIAN LIVING

The Ten Commandments of God

1. I, the Lord, am your God. You shall not have other gods besides me.
2. You shall not take the name of the Lord, your God in vain.
3. Remember to keep holy the sabbath day.
4. Honor your father and your mother.
5. You shall not kill.
6. You shall not commit adultery.
7. You shall not steal.
8. You shall not bear false witness against your neighbor.
9. You shall not covet your neighbor's wife.
10. You shall ot covet anything that belongs to your neighbor.

Duties of Catholics

Chief Precepts of the Church

1. To keep holy the day of the Lord's Resurrection: to worship God by participating in Mass every Sunday and holyday of obligation: to avoid those activities that would hinder renewal of soul and body, e.g., needless work and business activities, unnecessary shopping and so on.
2. To lead a sacramental life; to receive Holy Communion frequently and the Sacrament of Reconciliation regularly—mini-

mally, to receive the Sacrament of Reconciliation at least once
a year (only if a serious sin is involved); minimally also, to receive Holy Communion at least once a year between the First
Sunday of Lent and Trinity Sunday.

3. To study Catholic teaching in preparation for the Sacrament of
    Confirmation, to be confirmed, and then to continue to study
    and advance the cause of Christ.
4. To observe the marriage laws of the Church: to give religious
    training, by example and word, to one's children; to use parish
    schools and catechical programs.
5. To strengthen and support the Church: one's own parish
    community and parish priests, the worldwide Church and the
    Pope.
6. To do penance, including abstaining from meat and fasting
    from food on the appointed days.
7. To join in the missionary spirit and apostolate of the Church.

The Beatitudes

1. Blest are the poor in spirit: the reign of God is theirs.
2. Blest are the sorrowing: they shall be consoled.
3. Blest are the lowly: they shall inherit the land.
4. Blest are they who hunger and thirst for holiness: they shall
    have their fill.
5. Blest are they who show mercy: mercy shall be theirs.
6. Blest are the single-hearted: for they shall see God.
7. Blest are the peacemakers: they shall be called sons of God.
8. Blest are those persecuted for holiness' sake: the reign of God
    is theirs. (Mt 5:3-10)

The Seven Gifts of the Holy Spirit

Wisdom, Understanding, Counsel, Fortitude, Knowledge, Piety, Fear of the
Lord.

The Theological Virtues

FAITH is a gift by which the Holy Spirit helps us to accept
God's word and to give ourselves to the Father.
HOPE is a gift which helps us to know God that loves us and cares
for us and that we can trust in him.
LOVE is a gift which helps us to love God and to love all people for
the love of God because they too belong to him.

The Moral Virtues

P RUDENCE disposes us to form right judgments about what we
must do or not do.

JUSTICE disposes us to give everyone what belongs to him.

FORTITUDE disposes us to do what is good in spite of any difficulty.

TEMPERANCE disposes us to control our desires and to use rightly the things which please our senses.

Examination of Conscience

Did I accept the Christian challenge to do the most loving thing in each situation I was in? In the perspective of the great law of love consider the following commandments:

First Commandment:
   Have I neglected my morning or night prayers?
   Have I misbehaved at Mass?

Second Commandment
   Have I used God's name irreverently?

Third Commandment:
   Have I missed Mass through my own fault on Sundays or holydays?

Fourth Commandment:
   Have I disobeyed, angered, or been disrespectful toward my parents or teachers?

Fifth Commandment:
   Have I quarreled with or willfully hurt anyone?
   Have I refused to forgive?
   Have I caused another to commit sin?

Sixth and Ninth Commandments:
   Have I offended in any way by thought, word, or deed against the virtue of purity?

Seventh and Tenth Commandments:
   Have I stolen or destroyed property belonging to any other person?   Have I knowingly accepted stolen goods?

Eighth Commandment:
   Have I told lies or injured another person's character?

Capital Sins:
   Have I been angry, greedy, proud, envious, jealous, lazy. immodest, intemperate in eating or drinking?